Songs in the Night
A Witness to God's Love
in Life & in Death

Lucy Atkinson Rose

Compiled & Edited by
Ben Lacy Rose

cts
PRESS

Songs in the Night by Lucy Atkinson Rose
Compiled and Edited by Ben Lacy Rose

Cover design by David Skinner
Editorial assistance by
Nancy Graham Ogne and Sally Hicks

CTS Press
Decatur, Georgia

"God....who gives songs in the night"

Job 35:10

You are about to read the amazing story of a woman of uncommon faith who dealt with a gracious God with agonizing honesty.

Lucy had cancer, but in a very real sense the entries in her journal do not deal with the disease, but with God. Her journal records her struggle with God, the darkness and absence of God, the appearance of God in pure and unexpected moments, the grace of God, and the suffering of God in the pain of humankind like herself.

In her journey through pain, Lucy was enabled to experience the compassion of a benevolent God for her, but her vision included all those who suffer. It seems that her own suffering stretched her soul so large that it embraced the whole world.

As Lucy faced into her pain, the Spirit inspired her with visions and powerful metaphors of grace and hope. As she went into the darkness, she identified the place as the womb of God. In this special place of intimacy, she rested confident that all her needs would be met. To identify all these powerful metaphors would rob you of the surprise of discovery.

This earnest disciple, from the outset of her bout with cancer, is quite clear about her desire. She longed to live for the glory of God and die to the glory of God. Repeatedly she declared that she would like to live to see her daughter grow up and to grow old with her husband. But if this were not God's will, she desired God's glory above her own desire.

One of the refreshing aspects of these journal entries is the honesty with which Lucy deals with her guilt, her doubts, and her pain. Her words are not those of a hot-house believer, but a saint from the field who wades into the muck and mire of her own soul's struggle and tells us what it is like to suffer and have faith.

As this personal account of suffering and faithfulness unfolds, you are given the privilege of listening to and observing a saint in the making. "Sainthood" is a designation with which Lucy would have felt terribly uncomfortable. But that is the character of all saints. She relates to us progressively how a common person of faith engages her suffering, fear, and death in the confidence of our risen and living Lord.

Ben C. Johnson,   November 1997
Professor of Christian Spirituality,
Columbia Theological Seminary.

Preface by Editor/Compiler

Lucy wanted very much to live, and she had so much to live for. But, if God wanted her to witness to His love by her suffering and even dying, she was willing. She asked only that He give her *songs to sing in the night* -- and God did that, as this book shows.

Lucy's witness is presented here in four parts:

1. A **sermon** by Lucy in which she gives the essence of her faith--the faith that is spelled out in the journal, the letters and the conversations which follow. The sermon was preached in her home church, Clifton Presbyterian Church, Decatur, Georgia, on October 3, 1993, a few weeks after she learned that she had cancer and while she was undergoing chemotherapy.

2. Lucy's **journal** constitutes the main element of her witness here. When we knew that Lucy's cancer had returned and that she had a lot of suffering to endure, we urged her to keep a journal. The journal was written in longhand in a spiral-back notebook, and is here just as Lucy wrote it. We have inserted only the section headings that give the month and one of the songs that God gave in that month. We have left underlined in the journal and in the letters the words and phrases that she underlined.

3. Four **letters** by Lucy which were written to friends and family during the year after the cancer returned: July 1996 to July 1997.

4. The **record of Lucy's last five days** by Marilyn Washburn, a *special* friend who is a medical doctor and an ordained minister, and who attended Lucy to the very end.

The biographical sketch in the Appendix was composed by family members.

Ben Lacy Rose
Lucy's father

Contents

God leads His dear children along;
Some thro' the waters, some thro' the flood,
   Some thro' the fire, but all thro' the blood;
*Some thro' great sorrow, but **God gives a song**,*
   In the night season and all the day long.

Chapter 1

Sermon by Lucy Rose
The Man Born Blind

In John 9:1-3 we read, "As (Jesus) passed by, he saw a man blind from birth. And his disciples asked him, 'Rabbi, who sinned, this man or his parents, that he was born blind?' Jesus answered, 'It was not that this man sinned or his parents, but that the works of God might be manifested in him.'"

First I should tell you the story of my hat. It all began on a Monday back in June. I planned to work on my dissertation that day, but I decided to take a shower first. Then I thought while I was taking the shower that I would do one of those womanly things called "a self-exam;" and that is when I discovered the mass. I was too nervous to do anything on Monday. I hoped it would go away. On Tuesday I called around to find the cheapest mammogram in Atlanta. If you're interested, it's the DeKalb Medical Center. I was still hoping this mass would go away, so I let Wednesday go by. On Thursday I called and made an appointment for Friday.

I went and had the mammogram, and then they decided to do a sonogram also. I thought that was a bit unusual. The next thing I knew a very nice nurse was talking to me, but her badge said "Oncology." Now, I know that's a fancy name for cancer. Sure enough, the next week they told me it was cancer. I had a mastectomy, and now I'm in chemotherapy with my last treatment to be next Thursday. So I have only wisps of hair underneath this hat. Wigs are just too tight and too hot. I am told that my hair will come back, and that it may be curly when it does. So if you invite me back next year, you might not recognize me.

I tell you this story because I have found meaning in my experience this summer by laying my story next to the story in John 9:1-41 which I read and which Lisa told this morning.

Remember how the story goes: On seeing the man who was

9

born blind, the disciples asked Jesus, "Who sinned? This man or his parents that he was born blind?" Now, if he sinned, obviously it was before birth -- in the womb. Or perhaps it was his parents who were at fault and he was being punished. In those days sickness was interpreted as punishment for sin. So, who sinned?

In my own struggles with cancer I have read a few books. Not many. And each one assigns blame differently. One of the books implied that I was to blame: I hadn't eaten right; I hadn't exercised right; or I hadn't dealt with my stress properly. In fact, if I would begin eating right or exercising, I could heal myself. I even heard a TV advertisement on how to heal ourselves. Assigning blame to the person who suffers is still prevalent in our day.

Another book which I read assigned blame to our parents -- not just my parents, but to that whole generation who through public policy and through neglect allowed carcinogens into our food and toxic waste to seep into our streams and pollutants to belch into our atmosphere and create a world where cancer is so prevalent. It is my parents who are to blame!

But notice how different it is to assign blame, on the one hand, and on the other to ask the question the disciples asked. "Who sinned?" Their question implies that God is at work -- punishing sin, yes, but at least God is at work here. Whereas, in the modern day version of the question, there is no hint of God's activity, only "Who is to blame?"

So I found myself preferring the disciples' question-- reworded to be "How is God at work here?" And Jesus' answer makes sense, for he said, "No one sinned, not this man, not his parents. This man was born blind so that the works of God might be revealed in him."

Now in my own situation I knew that perhaps I had not lived a perfect life, and that there might be ways I could change my life for the better. And in fact I have tried to do some of that changing -- and I know that we should do something about the pollutants and the toxic wastes and the carcinogens in our food. But this only underlines all those questions again; and Jesus' answer is, "God is at work -- not a God who punishes but a God who saves."

10

The entire Gospel of John is about a God who "so loved the world that he gave his only begotten son" -- a God who sent his son into the world "not to condemn the world, but that the world through him might be <u>saved</u>." So I began to interpret my experience of the summer as an opportunity for the God of love to work works of healing and saving -- in my life.

Immediately after Jesus answered the disciples' question, he made mud of his spittle, put it on the man's eyes and sent him to the pool to wash. And he came back seeing. The people around asked, "Are you the man who used to beg? Are you the man who was born blind?" And he said, "Yes, yes, I am." But some of them said, "No. It's not him." And he kept saying, "Yes, yes. I am the one. And hear my story!" for now he has a story to tell -- of God's work in his life. He said, "A man anointed my eyes and I washed and now I see." In John's Gospel he tells his story at least three times. And by the last time he has gotten it down to the fewest words -- "I was blind and now I see." But he was still telling the story of God's work in his life. And I found the same thing true for my own life, as I looked for God's hand in it.

I'd like for us to go back to that Friday when I went home from the DeKalb Medical Center not knowing but feeling that I needed to get back into the Emory system and have an appointment with my own doctor. A cheap mammogram is one thing, but having your own doctor is another. So I went home that Friday afternoon and made an appointment with my doctor over at Emory. And then I worried, and then I prayed. Off and on the next days I spent a lot of time in silence and crying, wondering about what really mattered to me, wondering if this was a life-threatening experience. And in that quietness and through those tears I discovered three things about my life -- three wishes: I wanted to see my little girl, who is 4 years old, grow up; I wanted to move into old age with my husband; and I wanted to finish that dissertation. But underneath each of those, far deeper than those wishes, was my yearning to give glory to God's name. <u>That</u> was what I wanted, even if I could not have the others. And I found myself giving each one of those wishes to God. I wanted

11

so much to see my little girl grow up and I wanted to grow old with my husband by my side! How often I had put those two in God's hands when they went on a trip, or were driving around the town. I would say to God, "Take care of them. I want to be wrestling with you and to trust that you will bring me through this" -- but I had never put myself in God's hands and said, "God, if something happens to me, can I trust you to raise my little girl? Can I trust you to give her another mommy who will love her as I do? Can I trust you to raise her to be a child of yours, to give wisdom to my husband and to those who love her? And the same with my husband, can I trust you to give him the love he needs and will you open a future for him without me? Can I?" And each time I would say, "Yes. I can trust you, God, because I have trusted you throughout my life. And this dissertation -- I am committed to this dissertation. The ideas need to be out there in the world -- but I can give it to you, God." And there came over me through the course of that weekend a profound sense of peace, so that on Monday and Tuesday I found myself working on the dissertation with a great deal of energy.

And then on Wednesday I was in the clinic all day -- waiting and waiting -- waiting on doctors, waiting for the results of tests. And the Holy Spirit gave me a gift. I found myself singing -- not out loud -- but singing a hymn to myself over and over again, and it wasn't one I had consciously chosen:

"Have Thine own way, Lord! Have Thine own way!

Thou art the potter; I am the clay.

Mold me and make me after Thy will,

While I am waiting, yielded and still."

While I am waiting. While I am waiting, yielded and still.

About 3:00 o'clock in the afternoon we were told that it was cancer, and that the surgeon had an opening the next day. So I said, "I want a mastectomy. And I want it tomorrow." I had time to go back home and call Columbia Seminary and my church and the community that is important to me in my own neighborhood. I knew that I needed to be uplifted on the wings of prayer by them. Not as though those loved ones would change God's mind, but that they were

12

lifting me up and God was coming down and in the midst I would be sustained. The next day as I waited for the surgery, and as I was wheeled down that long hospital corridor toward surgery -- as I waited alone in the holding area, I was singing another song -- also a gift from the Holy Spirit -- and the first words on my mind as I woke up in the recovery room were the same hymn -- and the next day I continued to sing it:

"The lone, wild bird in lofty flight
Is still with Thee, nor leaves Thy sight.
And I am Thine! I rest in Thee.
Great Spirit, come and rest in me."

The surgery went well, and on Saturday the first words in my mind were still another song.

"To God be the glory through Jesus the Son.
I'll give God the glory, great things God has done.
Praise the Lord, Praise the Lord,
Let the earth hear your voice.
Praise the Lord,
Let the people rejoice.
To God be the glory through Jesus the Son.
I'll give God the glory, great things God has done."

I realized I had altered the words for inclusivity. What mattered, however, on that post-surgery morning was that I was singing praises to God who was at work in me.

Those were good days. I felt buoyed up. I felt the presence of the Spirit with me. And then came the chemotherapy. Days of nausea, days of exhaustion -- and slowly I found my spirit being ground down, depressed. I could no longer feel the buoyancy I had felt. I was discouraged, somewhat confused. And then, in preparing this sermon, I went back to the story about the man born blind. I was amazed. The biblical story does not have a happy ending. The man is thrown out of the synagogue.

Now think about that! He was not just being thrown out of church, but he was being excommunicated from the people of God forever. As a beggar, blind from birth, he had been on the margin of society -- but he had been on the margin. He had neighbors; he had family. But now he is outside the circle completely. Would he still have a loving family? Would he still have neighbors to speak to him and give him a few pennies? What would he do now that he could see and was not blind anymore? He couldn't go back to begging. And think about the long moments, maybe hours between the time he was kicked out of the synagogue and the time that Jesus found him -- in those hours I am sure he too felt confused and discouraged. And then Jesus found him and said, "Do you believe in the Son of man?" And he said, "Who is he that I may believe?" Jesus said, "I am he." And the man said, "I believe," and he worshiped him. And I too found that during those long, slow, empty days I could still believe, and worship.

I tell you these two stories today in order for you to believe through the stories of your own life -- in order for you to look at your own lives and the experiences that you have, and to ask, "Is God at work saving, loving, reaching out to me, to the whole world?" And can you believe and worship, particularly through those long, slow, empty days of confusion and disappointment?

The Bible story invites us to tell our story of God's work, and to believe and to worship. Amen.

Chapter 2

Journal of Lucy Rose
July 1996-April 1997

July: Near To The Heart of God

<u>July 5, 1996. Mystic CT</u> Am I ready to write this journal? Am I discerning God's timing? I'm not gung-ho about writing this. If my writing will bring glory to God's name, if anyone might come to trust God's love more deeply because of what I write, then I'm willing to write.

I've been wrestling with point of view. Do I write as I have in the past in my journals? Do I write letters to Lucy Mac? Do I fashion a story? There is a clue -- I don't want to <u>fashion</u> anything. I want to be an open vessel through which the writing comes. I want my conscious mind to stay in the background so that my heart can write, although there really are no longer a separate mind and a separate heart. There is one entity; "heart" describes it -- a heart that thinks.

Everybody's story is different. After my last bout with cancer, I got it wrong. I wanted to get back to living -- not living as it had been before, but living somehow as I thought life is. I was wrong. Now I realize <u>God is</u>; only <u>God</u> <u>is</u>. And life is God's gift.

<u>July 6, 1996. Mystic, CT.</u> Family reunion. Towel drying my hair in the bathroom I heard Lucy Mac outside ask someone about a picture of me. The someone answered that I had had long hair for a long time. In the background Mama was telling something funny. B and Nancy laughed and commented. I wasn't ready to join one of those groups or to disrupt the already conversations. I thought I'd take a few private minutes to write.

I want to capture something of the testimonial I gave at the

15

COH[1] and two nights ago with my family. And I hope there is a way to write things down as they happen.

The bone scan was on Tuesday in early June. Prior to that on Sunday and Monday my back was hurting so much that I could not do my sitting[2] in the rocking chair. So I lay down on the bed and tried to do my sitting in bed. Both nights I "fell" into a dark silent palpable sense of the love of God. I was engulfed in it. I was a fish and this was the life-giving substance in which I existed. That deep sense of the love of God carried me through the tears of the next few days. I felt no anger at God, no debilitating fear of the future or of death -- the bedrock feeling was being held in and being inseparable from the love of God.

I remember a couple of times after we learned of the cancer in my bones, closing my eyes to rest and a scary nightmarish something would come toward me. I remember saying with conviction, "I'm not afraid of you," and it disappeared.

I wasn't then and I don't feel now afraid of dying. I trust the words about Jesus in John's Gospel, "Jesus, knowing where he came from and where he was going...took a towel and began to wash the disciples' feet." I know I have come from God and I know I am going to God. How then do I live as a servant -- taking up the towel -- in the face of a possibly imminent death?

I appreciate those who call me on the phone and allow me to share my faith. They give me space to re-articulate the convictions and insights I'm writing here and there to test them to see if they are still real. The hardest calls are from those who are so distraught that my affirmations of faith seem to fall on deaf ears. But I must trust the Spirit to plant seeds. My task is only to surrender to the love of God.

That is my task, my job, my sole responsibility or thing to do. I am so addicted to doing and I make lists, check items off. I make

----

[1] Community of Hospitality, a group in Decatur with whom Lucy worked and from whom she received much support.

[2] She sometimes refers to her time of meditation as "sitting."

16

phone calls, write letters, work on my books...so that the doing takes over and becomes the chief end of my life; the doing rules my days and becomes a tyrannical dictator. I am convinced my only task each day is to surrender to the love of God I experienced during my sitting time before the bone scan. As I surrender to God, the things I need or think I need to do fall into place under God. My chief end is still to glorify and enjoy God. Making a phone call might -- probably does -- fit somewhere as a way of glorifying God. By my surrendering to God's love, the Spirit helps me with the phone call, the letter, the work on the books. I'm a long way from living this way regularly. But I have glimpses of it.

The bone scan was on Tuesday. Wednesday morning Gerry and I went in to talk to Dr. Peteet. We both like him; he was straight with us; he gave us time in the examining room to hold each other. We left the office and found ourselves crying in the parking garage. Silly me didn't want to have to pay money if we overstayed the limit the doctor's office had stamped for parking fees. We pulled ourselves together and drove to Candler Park where we cried and cried. I remember noticing how green everything was. When we felt stronger, we went home. That afternoon Ann Connor came over and stayed through supper. Currie came by. We sat on the porch and cried. Again I remember looking at the green trees and the bushes. Currie had a prayer -- Gerry, me, Lucy Mac, Dean, Ann and Currie holding hands.

The Wednesday night prayer group called "healing prayer" met. It was good to be among such friends.

Thursday I spent a good deal of time on the phone. Ann came over and did laundry. AB and Gerry ran errands; Lucy Mac played with Egan.

Friday Gerry and Lucy Mac dropped me at Green Bough[1] on their way to Florida.

---

[1] Green Bough is a retreat center at Adrian, Georgia, near Atlanta; Fay Key and Steve Bullinger are the directors.

At lunch and supper the table was set with heavy glass water glasses. I found them hard to pick up with one hand. At supper I remember eating the meal without drinking anything. Then I eased the glass to the front of the placemat, pushed the plate back and used two hands to lift the glass.

That night I was in pain when I went (at 11:30) for milk for taking my pills. I found I could walk with little pain if I bent over at the waist. Lynnsay's husband, Rob (both of them were staying at Green Bough), was in the lounge and I remember asking him please to pull a chair away from the table so I could sit down.

The next morning Ann Connor called to see how I was. I got up to go to the farm house with Steve, got about 10 steps from my door and crumpled in pain. I remembered before I fell to the floor that bending over allowed me to be mobile. I bent over, backed to my room and fell on the bed.

Fay and I had a good session on Friday afternoon. After the attempt to talk to Ann, I stayed in the retreat center and Fay and Steve brought my meals. I didn't go to Eucharist Saturday. I think I went to night-prayer, though. Fay and I had several conversations in my room but they weren't ordinary sessions. I had spent only a little time thinking/reflecting on passages. The pain was very intense and I couldn't get it down using the highest level of pain reliever dosage the doctor had allowed me. Gradually, however, the pain eased and by Tuesday I could walk upright.

On Friday Fay gave me Psalm 131 and Matthew 8:23-27. In the psalm I was struck by the sense of calmness -- "I have calmed and quieted my soul, like a weaned child" on its mother's breast. The Matthew passage also speaks of "a dead calm" (v.26). The third passage was Psalm 121. There I was struck by the order, God will keep our "going out" and our "coming in" (v.8). We are left "in." I thought the more normal order would be "in and out," maybe from the nursery rhyme "Go in and out the window." The psalm ends with "coming in." Sung by pilgrims, it expresses the hope of those traveling, those who have come out and are on the way. The hope is that God will bring them in to Jerusalem or to their homes. Sung or

18

read in church or synagogue, it expresses the affirmation of those whom God has once more brought in. I experience it as a hope that I can trust God to bring me to heaven's home.

The richest passage Fay gave me was II Cor. 4:7-18, "But we have this treasure in clay jars so that it may be made clear that this extraordinary power belongs to God and does not come from us. 8. We are afflicted in every way, but not crushed; perplexed, but not driven to despair; 9. persecuted, but not forsaken; struck down, but not destroyed; 10. always carrying in the body the death of Jesus, so that the life of Jesus may also be made visible in our bodies. 11. For while we live, we are always being given up to death for Jesus' sake, so that the life of Jesus may be made visible in our mortal flesh. 12. So death is at work in us, but life in you. 13. But just as we have the same spirit of faith that is in accordance with Scripture, 'I believed, and so I spoke' -- we also believe, and so we speak, 14. because we know that the one who raised the Lord Jesus will raise us also with Jesus, and will bring us with you into his presence. 15. Yes, everything is for your sake, so that grace, as it extends to more and more people, may increase thanksgiving to the glory of God. 16. So we do not lose heart. Even though our outer nature is wasting away, our inner nature is being renewed day by day 17. For this slight momentary affliction is preparing us for an eternal weight of glory beyond all measure, 18. because we look not at what can be seen but at what cannot be seen; for what can be seen is temporal, but what cannot be seen is eternal."

It is clear to me that grace -- as an extraordinary power from God and not from me -- is keeping me from feeling crushed, driven to despair, forsaken, or destroyed. Someone said to me on the phone, "You must be devastated." "No," I said; "Grace," I thought.

Verse 14 ("Knowing that he who raised the Lord Jesus will raise us also with Jesus and bring us with you into his presence") I like because it indicates Paul was sure that in Jesus' presence he and the Corinthians would be distinct personalities -- would be themselves -- not drops of water returning to the ocean.

Verse 16 ("So I do not lose heart. Though our outer nature is wasting away, our inner nature is being renewed day by day") is

19

very meaningful to me as I surrender daily, hourly -- moment by moment -- to God's love. I do feel that I am being renewed day by day.

I don't understand the verses about carrying the death of Jesus in my body so that the life of Jesus might be visible in my body. I keep meditating on those words. I can't see the life of Jesus in my mortal flesh. And am I carrying the death of Jesus in my body to the extent that I am willing to walk through or into the valley of the shadow of death willingly if the faith, hope and love of others is strengthened? There is a mysticism here I want to explore.

I'll leave some space for the other Scripture passages. I also did a bit of writing at Green Bough but not much.

First prayer times: Psalm 131, Psalm 121, Mark 4:35-41.

Second prayer times: Psalm 46, Psalm 138, II Cor. 4:7-18.

Third prayer times: II Cor. 4:7-18, Psalm 16, Psalm 17:8.

Fourth prayer times: Psalm 116, Rom. 8:18-31, Isaiah 30:15.

Lucy Mac and I have had some marvelous conversations about heaven. Some time ago she decided that whenever people were going to die -- including murder -- (I heard that as sudden death), God knows the person is going to die and lets that person know. That way the person is sure there is a room prepared so that she/he won't have to wait outside or move in with a friend for a night or two.

Sunday night Gerry and I shared our story at COH. We came to Peggy's to the Rose reunion on Monday. We shared our story here Wednesday night after everyone had gotten here.

July 8, 1996. Decatur, GA. I'm really clear I'm trying to interpret my own story and no one else's. My convictions about God are my own and I don't mean to imply they are anyone else's.

Another psalm Fay gave me to meditate on is Psalm 46. The theme of calmness is repeated there. I read it this morning for Gerry's and my devotions and I was struck by how noisy it is:

-the earth changing, the mountains shaking in the sea, the waters roaring and foaming, the mountains trembling in tumult (vv. 2-3);

-the nations in an uproar, kingdoms tottering, God speaking so that

20

the earth melts (vv. 6-7);

-the breaking of the bow, the shattering of the spear, the burning shields (chariots) -- hear the roaring, crackling fire -- so much noise!

Then "Be still, and know that I am God": even the exulting of verse 10b could be noisy shouts of praise -- but in the midst of it all, a stillness, a calm, in which we know God and experience God as refuge. Here and in Psalm 131 we calm ourselves. In Psalm 131 the calm follows the trauma of weaning, and in Psalm 46 the calm accompanies a turning in the midst of the trauma. In Matthew 8:26 ("Then Jesus rebuked the wind and the sea, and there was a great calm") Jesus creates a dead calm with his rebuke to the winds and the sea. There is a paradox -- who is responsible for the calmness? Us or Jesus? Like the chicken and the egg -- once in the cycle you can't say -- chicken implies egg which implies chicken. We calm ourselves because the word of Jesus is already at work within us. This word lives in us so that by the power of God, by the life already alive within us, we can calm and quiet our souls turning toward the one who is already refuge.

Surely the one who can utter a voice so that the earth melts (v.6) can speak a word and melt the cancer cells in my body. Daddy this week reminded me of the words of Shadrach, Meshach and Abednego to Nebuchadnezzar. The gist of their words is, "Our God is able to deliver us from the fiery furnace and out of your hand, O King. But if he does not, be it known to you, O King, that we will not serve your gods and we will not worship the statue you have set up" (Dan. 3:17-18). God is able. And if God does not utter the word and melt the cancer away inside me, I will by grace still be faithful. Because God is love, and I surrender to the love of God that has surrounded me, encircled me, washed through me and claimed me. If God does not, God has reasons far beyond my limited understanding, reasons that will result in grace extending to more and more people, and in increasing thanksgiving to the glory of God (II Cor. 4:15). That is my hope and my joy and my all -- glorifying God in life and death, by my living and dying. By God's grace I will be faithful to God even if God does not deliver me from the cancer.

21

One morning while in Connecticut, I think it was Monday night, I dreamed that I died and was in heaven. Looking down at the earth I saw that Lucy Mac and Gerry hadn't made it; they were homeless on the streets. I went to God and began beating on God's chest, crying hysterically, "You lied! You're not the God you led me to believe in. You lied." Then something switched in me and I realized that even if God is not a God of love whom I can trust with myself and with Lucy Mac, Gerry, Dean and Louie as God's baptized children, even if there is no heaven or loving God into whom we find ourselves gathered after death -- I will keep on believing as though it were true. With this God in whom I trust, I find peace, calm, stillness, even joy.

I want to read some of what is being written about God and suffering. One of my hypotheses is that much of it is written from the perspective of God as separate, as Other. If God is separate Other and powerful, love slips aside and God can (does?) manipulate people like chess pieces. If God is separate Other and love, then God's power gets redefined. But if God is mystically attached to us, inseparable from us, or we part of God, identical to that of us which is eternally alive -- then the relationship among power, love and suffering gets reconfigured. After I fell into the all-engulfing love of God, I found myself in love with God -- so in love I would follow this God anywhere; accompany this God through any experience. Just to be with this Love is enough, is joy. Suffering (Is what I'm experiencing suffering? I wonder.) somehow is on behalf of love -- love not only for me (on behalf of meaning in my life) but also for the world of others (on behalf of God's promised shalom). One time I found myself remembering the love song, "I will follow him. Ever since he touched my hand, I knew, I knew him my own love to be, and nothing can keep him from me; he is my destiny." Silly song, but somehow true of how I feel about God.

Another song I've been singing is, "There is a place of quiet rest, near to the heart of God. A place of all on earth most blessed, near to the heart of God. O Jesus, blessed Redeemer, near to the heart of God, hold us who wait before thee, near to the heart of God."

22

Ann Connor's gift song was, "Our God, our help in ages past. Our hope for years to come. Our shelter from the stormy blast, and our eternal home." We sang it Wednesday night after Gerry and I shared with the family in Connecticut.

July 10, 1996. This morning Gerry and I read Psalm 91 for devotions. Two promises impressed themselves on me (vv.. 15 and 16). One "I will be with them in trouble," and two, "I will rescue them and honor them; with long life I will satisfy them and show them my salvation." These promises point backward to earlier verses and previous promises. 1. God will deliver you from the snare of the fowler and from the deadly pestilence (v.3). What pestilence is more deadly than cancer? 2. Because you have made the Lord your refuge, the Most High your dwelling place, no evil shall befall you, nor scourge come near your tent (vv.. 9-10). Was it Walter Brueggemann who called the cancer evil? Is it? Or is evil the despair and faithlessness the cancer threatens to bring in its wake? Is cancer a scourge? Verses 5 and 6 are different promises. So far God has kept these promises protecting me from <u>fear</u> of the terror of the night, the arrow that flies by day, the pestilence that stalks in darkness, the destruction that wastes at noonday. One thing I know -- I do live in the shelter of the Most High, I do abide in the shadow of the Almighty, I do say and, if I haven't used these exact words, I do so now, "My refuge and my fortress; my God, in whom I trust" (v. 2). So, what about the promise? Again, there are two kinds. One, God has kept and is keeping -- freedom from fear and God's presence in this time of trouble. And what of the other? Verse 3 could be read that the fowler's snare <u>has</u> caught the bird or that the deadly pestilence has claimed its victim and that God <u>delivers</u> from sure death. The same can be the reading of verses 15a and 16, that the singer of the psalm is <u>rescued</u> from an early death and given long life.

In each case, and in my own, the fulfillment of the promise is still in the future. God may still release me from the fowler's snare, snatch me from the clutches of the deadly pestilence, rescue me and honor me with long life. That is my prayer each morning.

23

Like the woman in Luke 18:1-8, I feel commissioned to pray and pray and pray. How much more will God, who loves me and protects me, hear my cry. But the promise in Luke 18 is that God will grant justice -- maybe as God sees with the eyes of eternity, justice that issues in shalom is better served by my testimony unto death, a death that is not delayed. If so, the key to my praying is remaining faithful, keeping faith in God's love and in God's promise of shalom. I keep praying, not finally to receive a "Yes" answer to my prayer, but to do my part in keeping my faith alive and vital.

So I pray for God to say the word that melts my cancer -- but I rest in God, my refuge -- in God, not in the hope of Yes-answered prayers.

The night Gerry and I shared our story with COH, Ann prayed a prayer over us as the gathered community laid hands on us. At some point she read Habakkuk 3:17-19. So far they are true words: "Though the fig tree does not blossom, and no fruit is on the vines; though the produce of the olive fails and the fields yield no food, though the flock is cut off from the fold and there is no herd in the stalls, yet I will rejoice in the Lord, I will exult in the God of my salvation. God, the Lord, is my strength. God makes my feet like the feet of a deer, and makes me tread on the heights."

Psalm 91 makes two promises and I pray for the fulfillment of both. Nevertheless, if God says "No" to deliverance, rescue and long life, still will I cling to God for refuge, resting beneath God's protective wings; still will I rejoice in God's presence that is protecting me from debilitating fear; still I will praise God who is my strength today and my salvation both in life and death, both in my living and in my dying.

I have only in the last day or two been able to do my sitting again in a way that feels life-giving. In the past few weeks I've felt scattered, unfocused, empty of God's stillness whenever I tried to meditate. Some times I found myself drifting into a day-dream from which I could not draw myself back. Though there have been lots of day-dreams and even night-dream type images, there have been few "visions" that have felt like gifts from God, particularly visions about

24

the cancer. There have been only those four. Two began at Green Bough. Dr. Peteet had told me that the pain might escalate as the tamoxifen went to work on the cancer. So as the pain arose, often localized in a particular area of my back, I envisioned charwomen with scrub brushes scrubbing the bones clean. The pain was from their scrubbing hard to clean each area thoroughly. Each day there was a new area of focus; lower right back, lower middle right back, upper middle right back, upper right back One day the pain moved to the upper left back but it quit there. Accompanying this visualization (although I never really saw these women) was a hand I did "see" that sprinkled each area with holy water, and while the hand sprinkled holy water (I think using some leafy branch -- hyssop? -- that had been dipped in holy water) words of blessing were spoken over the bone area and over the cancer. I was shocked that the blessing included a blessing for the cancer. One time the blessing was said with clear words that emerged full-blown into my conscious mind -- though I have long since forgotten them. The rest of the time I simply saw the hand sprinkling the holy water and felt the blessing.

Sometime yesterday, and I think, maybe last night, I got a very quick glimpse of a cancer area. It was as though I stood at the top of an escalator that disappeared into darkness way down into the tunnel. Little somethings were pushing and shoving, though not violently, just steadily going up and down. Some of them I think were carrying suitcases and I remember thinking, "I wonder if they are going somewhere."

This morning I had a fourth brief vision. All I remember (though there wasn't much else to the vision) is a broom sweeping up into a pile ant-sized dead black things.

On Wednesday afternoon in Connecticut I told Lucy Mac that Gerry and I were going to share with the whole family about my being sick. She said, "Boring," and when the time came took some toys to her room. After a little while, Gerry was still sharing facts about the cancer and what the doctor had said, she appeared at the door. Making her way around to me she slipped me a post-on note that said, quoting something Gerry had just said, "Lucy's sprit (spirit?) has been

25

the main part of the family." I smiled at her and received two more notes about writing her a "mistry" (e.g. mystery) apparently about myself, she told me. I think I discouraged her and postponed that request and then it was time for me to share how I have been coping with the cancer. Abruptly I ceased being her communication partner. Next thing I was aware of with her was that she had handed me a note saying, "Lucy, let them share their love." And she was crawling under tables and behind chairs to hand notes to everyone in the room. The ones to Gerry and me were similar. The notes to the others had each person's name, then the message, "Share your love with them." Because of that note Tom was emboldened to share tearfully of his mother's dying from cancer just about two years ago. Her faith had not been strong and he was grateful for Gerry's and my witness to God's love and promises, and for our willingness to include the whole family in our journey. Once again I was reminded of God's using messengers of all ages and sizes to speak a holy word -- out of the mouths of babes and infants.....a little child shall lead them. Lucy Mac is not always an angel. But she was that night.

July 12, 1996. Dear God, I want to stay in the very center of your will -- your love -- as though I were living in the eye of the hurricane.

This morning for devotions I read to Gerry Psalm 102. Several verses really struck me hard and brought tears to my eyes. I choked them out. Vv. 23-24 "(God) has broken my strength in midcourse; (God) has shortened my days. 'O my God,' I say, 'Do not take me away at the mid-point of my life; you whose years endure throughout all generations.'" Precisely my prayer. Maybe at 49 years I'm a little over the mid-point of my life, but I do feel as though I would like to live several more decades, and God, who is eternity, surely has years to spare. And so I cry to the Lord, the Creator of all that is, the one who endures when all else crumbles, withers, rots and disappears from the earth -- I cry to this God because my bones burn like a furnace in my back (v.3), because my days seem like an evening shadow as I wither away like grass (v.11), because Scripture promises God regards the prayer of the destitute and will not despise our prayer

26

(v.17), because God is a God who sets free those who are doomed to die so that God's name may be declared in Zion, and God's praise in Jerusalem when peoples gather together and kingdoms, to worship the Lord (vv.20-22). That is my prayer for myself that whether I live by the grace of God who sets me free from imminent death or whether I die by the grace of God who keeps me faithful unto death, the name of the Lord may be declared throughout the earth, wherever God's covenant people worship so that a people yet unborn may praise the Lord (vv.18, 22). And my prayer for Gerry, Lucy Mac, Dean and Louie is that they may live secure and be established in God's presence (v.28).

What does Paul mean in Philippians 1:20-21 when he writes, "It is my eager expectation and hope that I will not be put to shame in any way, but that by my speaking with boldness, Christ will be exalted now as always in my body, whether by life or by death. For to me, living is Christ...." I sort of understand the end of verse 21, "Dying is gain," but what does "Living is Christ" mean and how is Christ exalted in my body? Through my speaking -- using my mouth, brain, heart, soul?

A few days ago Lucy Mac and I were reading Someday Heaven for the second time -- her choice. Early in the book is a claim that the reader can be sure his or her name is written in the Book of Life so that he or she will go to heaven, and the reader's attention is directed to the end of the book and a prayer for giving one's life to Jesus. Lucy Mac was interested, so we turned to the back of the book and I read the prayer. Then I told her she needn't say those exact words and in fact she already belongs to God because of her baptism. But, I went on, one day she will have to claim God's love for her for herself. And we don't surrender to God just once but over and over again. In fact, I told her, I had lately been surrendering myself to God many times every day. "Oh?" she looked at me. "Why?" "Because I've been so sick," I answered. "Well," she mused, "then the cancer has done some good."

July 15, 1996. Tonight I had a delightful conversation with Oo

27

Finkner. We laughed -- I don't laugh enough. I was amazed to hear myself saying -- if I had a choice between continuing on just as life had been before the news a month ago and going through the catastrophe of the last month so that I am the person I am today, I think I'd choose the latter. And I think I'm telling the truth.

July 22, 1996. I preached yesterday at Doris Chandler's ordination. If the tape Lauren made doesn't turn out, I'll try to recreate the sermon. It was a pretty good summary of where I am at this stage of the pilgrimage.

This morning I've been reading Enduring Grace, the section on Teresa of Avila. There are several sections I want to reflect on as well as a passage in the Catherine of Genoa section. I want to grow in my practice of two of Catherine of Genoa's "nevers": "Never say, I will or I will not. Never say mine; but always say ours" (144). Flinders comments "Standard issues, these practices for the spiritual aspirant of any time or place -- simple, yet powerful strategies aimed to reduce, little by little, the tyranny of 'I' and 'mine.'" (144).

The passages in the Teresa of Avila section on which I want to reflect describe the four ways we can water the seeds God plants within us. These descriptions provide clues about my concern that, as my life settles into a routine and returns to familiar activities, I not lose the peace and joy I've experienced being so intentionally in God's presence. But!! Maybe that shouldn't be my concern or maybe I have not articulated my concern properly. Losing the peace and joy I now experience wouldn't be so bad if I remained faithful to God. I think my concern is that I not regress; that's what I feel I did to some extent last May -- I regressed to a state of frenzied activity in which the activity and the pace drove out of my heart and living all realization that God is my sole preoccupation -- everything -- everything is secondary or tertiary. As I move from "crisis mode," my description of how I was living before the trip to Connecticut, to -- how should I describe this new mode? --living mode, I pray from the depths of my heart and bowels that I not regress, that I not turn away from living in fellowship with God.

28

Now to the summaries of ways Teresa says we can water our holy plants -- or ourselves as holy plants/seedlings. One, drawing water from the well. The dangers to be overcome are distractedness and weariness. The watchword is determination. All of that rings true for me of my living as described in my sermon about living water and of my sitting for the last three years. Sometimes I couldn't find the well; so often I would get distracted and overcome with weariness. Over the last six weeks my sitting has had a different character -- often a distractedness that I set down to the medicine. I could not concentrate. As I have cut back on the pain medication, I have found myself resting in darkness, often overstaying the 20-minute time limit. No longer are there inspired fantasies or day-dreams, at least not in the past few days. Only full, gentle life-giving darkness of the divine womb (178).

Teresa's second way involves a water wheel and a system of aqueducts. Our task is to turn the crank of the waterwheel. Phrases that describe this mode are "the prayer of quiet," "the soul has begun to be recollected," "the water is higher," "grace (water) is more clearly manifest to the soul" (178). I suppose this mode would describe my sitting in those moments when God seemed to be answering the yearnings of my heart -- when sitting was not hard work and routine repetition, but heart-restoring nourishment.

The third way water gets into the garden is from a river or spring. This too, I began to understand and preached about in the living water sermon. Now God is the gardener, the soul is given over entirely to God; this mode of watering is accompanied by joy. I have had glimpses of this mode of watering. Several expressions I don't understand. I'll write them down for meditation. The joy of this mode of watering is "a delightful disquiet" (178). Why disquiet? And, "The prayer here is 'a sleep of the faculties,' wherein 'the water of grace rises up to the throat of this soul.'" I guess the sleep of the faculties takes all the "doing" off of the one meditating. All attention of the heart, soul and strength turn to God. Two other descriptions of this mode of watering are intriguing to me. One, this mode of watering produces fruit which can be distributed to others, "with God's

29

permission" (fascinating qualifiers!). And -- this mode of watering nourishes a soul that can be engaged both in the contemplative and the active life. I guess I knew something of this during my sitting times; often -- no, sometimes -- my sitting left me with images or visions that I have shared with others, and my sitting definitely began to spill over into my active life. In the last few weeks I have been keenly aware of God the Gardener during my active moments, although I must admit that my active moments have been very quiet and restful compared to last spring. My sitting time has been a full emptiness. My active time has been an engaged awareness of God (in my better moments, at least).

The fourth way of watering the garden, the holy seedling that is myself, is union. Teresa equates this with rainfall that "soaks and saturates this entire garden" (179). Here Teresa claims, "The soul becomes so courageous that if at that moment it were cut in pieces for God, it would be greatly consoled. Such prayer is the source of heroic promises...the beginning of contempt for the world" (179). I have had moments of experiencing this kind of abandonment to God. I am convinced that as the cancer causes me and others to glorify God, I can rejoice in it (or is that too strong?) -- embrace it without anger or bitterness or fear, while still praying that God say the word that will melt it away. I have not made any heroic promises, however, and my contempt for the world is ambiguous. I am more thankful for and aware of the beauty of God's creation -- especially greens -- though the sunset last night made my heart overflow with awe and wonder. And I am more at one with the people around me and those whose paths I cross by means of brief unexpected encounters, e.g. on the street corner when the man asked me for money. I am somehow deeply bonded to all people -- I do not have contempt for them. But I do have contempt -- at least the beginnings of contempt for many of the values of the world or "the world" as it constitutes the realm at odds with God's shalom. Such contempt is tricky business, not simple or clear-cut. The description I resonate with most deeply is Teresa's expansion of the metaphor of rainfall. "If the soil is well cultivated by trials, persecutions, criticisms, illness (Wow!), and if it is softened by living in great detachment from self-interest (I have a long way to go) the water soaks it to the extent that it is almost never dry. But (this is the part that stirs my concerns and throws me back on the necessity of the Gardener's constant attention) it is still hardened in the earth. (Do not harden my heart, O God, but take from me my heart of stone and give me a heart of flesh.) And has a lot of briers...and is still not removed from occasions (to sins) the ground will dry up again" (179). (By your grace, O God, may the soil of my garden not dry up again. Guard me from the cares and pleasures of the world, that surrendering to your care and bearing fruit for your shalom may be my only concerns. May I surrender all other concerns to you.)

July 23, 1996. Here I began reading Teresa of Avila's Interior Castle. No I or my, no me or mine. There is only ours...and thine. To use the language of Teresa is the purpose of my sitting, the recollection of the soul and the necessary accompanying recollections of the "faculties" -- which I take to be the senses. (Teresa also writes of the faculties of the soul.) Teresa writes of "the most secret things that pass between God and the soul" in the central mansion (10). I like the idea that one enters the castle by prayer and meditation. Once on the inside, the soul (?) "must be allowed to roam through these mansions" (11), except that one must spend a long time in the mansion where one acquires humility.

July 24, 1996. I found myself praying tonight, "Dear God, help me with my back" -- what I meant was that I have a plan, a hope for weaning myself from the MS Contin or at least from most of it. In the midst of that prayer I found myself saying, "No, dear God, I surrender my back and its pain to you."

At healing prayer tonight when I tried to articulate my desire to keep something of the last 6 weeks as I move from extraordinary time to ordinary time, Woody made me mad or upset by comparing me to Peter, wanting to build a booth on the mount of transfiguration. The image has stuck with me. I don't think I want to stay on the mount, but instead I want to keep the memory of epiphany close by

31

and to remember that epiphany belongs to every place and time.

July 26, 1996. Started The Cloister Walk. Several concepts struck me: the liturgy of the hours is about "the sanctification of time" (xiii); time as God's gift; each day there is time for prayer, work, study, play; liturgical time is poetic time willing to wait attentively on stillness rather than pushing to get the job done (xiii); Benedict knows that practicalities -- the order and times for psalms to be read, care of tools, the amount and type of food and drink and clothing -- are also spiritual concerns (7); Benedict's words, "Keep death before your eyes" (8).

July 30, 1996 AM. I've been very sleepy since last night. Yesterday I got my medication all mixed up, took Megace instead of ib and MS Contin around 3:30; I've done that twice lately. But yesterday I forgot to take the ib and MS Contin till after supper. So the pain in my back gradually escalated despite a Roxicet. And I pulled something in my front ribs -- the right side about 5 days ago, the left side day before yesterday, so the costrochondritis pain is back. I think as the pain increased, my good spirits waned. I found myself crying as I did my exercises on the floor in the computer room listening to the Olympics. Then when I finally lay down, I found myself in the midst of another crying bout. I kept saying, "I surrender to your love, God," over and over amidst sobs. Then I asked God if there were anything I should do or do differently, if God wanted me to follow the alternative medicine regimen of herbs that Becky sent or go to Mexico, to let me know -- through a dream or whatever means. The only dream that came is very sketchy and not an answer to my petition. Some people were looking for Gerry and me -- at the end of the dream they found us -- what I remember is that things were okay because we were together. I don't remember any panic or fear.

 PM. My sister, Peggy, left this mid-day. It has been a wonderful visit and we organized my 2/3rds of the computer room, as well as my dresser top. We didn't make it to school. She'll come back in September to help me organize my office there. I think something about the thought of going to school threw me in a funk. Peggy sensed it and had an epiphany moment of her own yesterday. So this morning, following her suggestion that we do something to ritualize our transition moments, the three of us -- Peggy, Gerry and I -- held a prayer service. After a call to worship of scattered verses from Psalm 46, Peggy shared her sense of being in transition; then the three of us prayed for her and her concerns. Then I tried to put into words the source of my tears and the essence of this move from crisis mode to living/return-to-work mode. One of the issues that surfaced was that I've been battling the "work-is-everything" ethos at school very much on my own. School brings out a certain stress-filled, maybe fearful, part of me and I have tried to keep that part integrated with my at-home self, my "sitting" self through using the water over which I've said the baptismal prayer, and crossing myself with the words, "I am baptized with water and Spirit. I have been buried and raised to new life in Christ." That was my ritual every day as I entered my office last year. And, if I were going to stay in the office a while, I would light the oil lamp with words like, "Holy space, holy time, holy work, holy worker." Anyway, those rituals and the Tuesday lunch group that talked about discipleship were the ways I tried to make working at school somewhat spiritual. But toward the end of last semester, the pace was so frenetic, worse than it has ever been. One of the suggestions that Gerry made this morning was that he would be willing to support me more in my attempts to counter the workaholic ethos of the seminary. I want to adopt a more Benedictine pattern -- time every day for prayer, work, study, play. I thought maybe I can get the healing prayer group to pray with me over the water I use, so I could think of their support as I call upon God's help each day I enter the office. And if Gerry and I pray about my spiritual state at school every morning during our devotions when I'll be going to school, maybe, maybe my being and working at school can be holy.

I need to write a letter to all the wonderful folks who are praying for me. Maybe I can start it now: Dear_____, Thanks for your card, note, letter, phone call, gift. No, that won't work. I don't think it's time yet.

July 31, 1996. I just finished reading the second chapter of the fourth mansions in Teresa of Avila's Interior Castle. I found it very thought-provoking. Her calling God "His Majesty" respects God's transcendence and sovereignty. As I try to articulate my experiences and reflections on those experiences in this sickness, I don't want to ignore my grounding in Calvin and my deep belief in God's sovereignty. I also found myself reminded that the feelings that have accompanied the last 6 or 7 weeks are gifts, favors from God, not to be expected or depended on.

Several phrases and sections seem noteworthy to me. Teresa claims that one of our desires is "to have fruition of His Majesty." Are we Marys or vines bringing forth the fruit of God? Here Teresa describes the two ways of watering: by conduits and by God's direct favor. The conduits imply our efforts, including meditation. The other fountain is directly connected to the source, God. The result is "the greatest peace and quietness and sweetness within ourselves" (81). The basin fills and overflows and reaches even the body, "the whole of the outer man" (81). She quotes Psalm 118:32 (AV 119:32) as saying that the heart enlarges. I want to look that up. She continues, "I do not think that this happiness has its source in the heart at all. It arises in a much more interior part, like something of which the springs are very deep; I think this must be the center of the soul" (82).

There are many more striking passages I won't record here. She ends with the admonition not to strive for God's favors and consolations. One of five reasons is "because the true preparation for receiving these gifts is a desire to suffer and to imitate the Lord, not receive consolation; for, after all, we have often offended Him" (84). The desire to suffer is foreign to me.

August: On Eagle's Wings

Aug. 4, 1996. Didn't do a good job of sitting (meditating) this morning at all. First Gerry came down and talked to me about the downside of Olympic tournament competition. Then he made me some chicken noodle soup. It tasted good after two days of being sick

-- three, really. The doctor thinks it is a gastrointestinal virus. I was sick as a dog Friday, but at least the hardness in my intestines from backed-up feces is gone. So I can praise God now even if I hated being so sick. I haven't been able to take the Megace or ibuprofen since Friday morning when I started throwing up. I guess I'll just have to leave my back pain (not much -- a sore neck) and the cancer full in God's hands.

PM. I need to eat on Green Bough time. Regular time is fast -- make the next bite while chewing the first. Green Bough time is slow -- eat one bite, wait, take the bite, sometimes put the spoon down, "taste and see that the Lord is good." Then make the next bite.

PM. My lower back and neck are aching. My temperature is 101.4°. I feel almost back to square one -- at Green Bough pain.

Aug. 5, 1996. Got up this morning at 6:30 to try and get a couple or three crackers in my very empty stomach -- plus an ibuprofen and a Megace. I ate -- nibbled down -- two crackers in 14 minutes for each one. That's Green Bough time. I'd like to live that slowly all the time. The third cracker also took 14 minutes but I think I did that on purpose.

PM. I cried tonight. I don't want to die, and I ache in my neck and back. Gerry held me. I love him so -- and Lucy Mac. God has been so good to me. I never ever thought I'd find someone I'd love like Gerry or have a daughter as delightful and sometimes wonderfully difficult -- as Lucy Mac. God has been so good. I know God hasn't abandoned me -- Gerry agrees.

Aug. 8, 1996. I've written diary entries in my head for the last two days but have been too weak to pick up the pen. Like the chemotherapy experience, it's been hard to experience the active, attentive-toward-me presence of God I experienced before I got sick last Thursday. Yet many times I've visualized myself as a tiny fish in the ocean of God -- from the ocean I draw all I need. In the ocean I can rest. A few times I've been a fetus in God's womb where it is warm, dark, safe. They were good moments but fleeting.

35

The doctor's office called to say that the hepatitis test came back negative. Now I have to go for a CT of the liver Monday.

Gerry's dad is in the clinic at Penney Farms, FL. Lucy Mac and I talked about the possibility of his dying. I told her that when some people die, they seem to see heaven and how beautiful it is. She responded, "That's good."

I've received lots of cards and letters in the last few days. Mostly from new people. Paul Franklyn wrote something about the prayers of so many and who knows what can happen in sacred space. I really felt his words move me deeply -- prayers create sacred space.

PM. There's an image I forgot to write down. I think it came to me this morning during my sitting-meditation time. I was in an antechamber to the throne room. Double doors three stories high stood before me. Everything was gold and ornate. The room was circular with a seat running from the edge of the door around the room to the opposite edge of the door. I was waiting to be ushered into God's presence. And I wasn't waiting patiently. I was impatiently pacing up and down or sitting anxiously in one spot along the wall, only to jump up and move to another seat.

I have just begun reading Ann Weems's Psalms of Lament. The introduction implies that the only posture that is faithful is banging on the door, aggressively demanding God's attention. I believe they would call my surrendering to God's love "docility." But it fits for me -- I'm not angry or aggressive. At the same time Abb's first psalm invites me to speak to God of my pain, my fears, my sadness. Is it better to lose "the one you love better than your own life," or to anticipate your own death, leaving behind the ones you love more than your own life?

The pain in my back has been intense today. That scares me. I took 2 mild pain pills and the pain has backed off somewhat.

Aug. 12, 1996. In my sitting just now I realized I'm waiting for the One my soul and heart love more deeply than I love my own life. I must reread the Song of Solomon.

The throne room doors opened and I got on my hands and

knees, unable to move. A voice said, "Come," and I crawled forward a little, face to the ground out of shame. Then God picked me up and held me to the divine bosom and said, "In the darkness I hold you and cradle you and infuse you. Love the darkness."

Aug. 15, 1996. I've lost most of the sense of being connected to others and to the created world. Lately my meditating has been very solitary -- a lone fish in the dark sea, a solitary waiter in the anteroom to God's throne room. I've tried to remember that my pain unites me with all those in pain -- all those who suffer physically or emotionally. Sometimes I remember.

As I was doing my back exercises last night and this morning, I found myself entrusting myself physically to God. I'm not trying to regain control of my body or trying to figure out a way to beat the pain on my own. I am trying to work with God for that measure of life and health God has already determined for me. Unless the Lord build the house, the laborers labor in vain. The medicine, the exercise, the rest -- all are surrendered to God. The doctor on Tuesday began to talk about chemotherapy; he's not convinced the Megace is working. I found myself discouraged -- tears welled up on the X-ray table. I realize I'd placed my hope in the Megace -- it was going to work for ten years. But my hope is only in God -- each day is God's gift.

Life has slowed way down. I get up around 7:30 for a Megace and ibuprofen. Then I do my sitting till around 8:00. Sometimes I go back to bed; today I did my morning exercises. Afterward Lucy Mac and Gerry were up so I ate cereal with them. About 9:00 I went back to bed for an hour. Then I got up about 10:00, showered, and read most of a chapter in Newbegin's Foolishness to the Greeks, which we'll use in the "Baptism and Evangelical Identity" course. Joy Pruett came by for a visit about 11:30, my first morning visitor. Then I ate lunch with Dean and read a chapter in Teresa of Avila and Cloister Walk. Now Lucy Mac wants me to play a game with her. I'm expecting one, maybe two, visitors this afternoon. Tonight Gerry wants to go to Salem Campground for singing and maybe a service. I might have to take two chairs so I'll be able to sit comfortably. I hope I can keep a slow pace like this even when I go back to school.

Aug. 16, 1996. The doctor called today to say two blood indicators were up, meaning the cancer wasn't being contained in the bone or is active or something. He's ready to move to chemotherapy. I've made up my mind I'll try it for Lucy Mac's and Gerry's sakes, and Dean's and Louie's. But I'm disappointed.

Last night I did go with Gerry and Lucy Mac to the Salem Campground. We met AB and Ann, Egan and Rebekah there. Tom Long turned out to be the preacher on the Luke 18 text -- Jesus told them a parable to the effect that they should pray always and not lose heart. His examples of losing heart included "the cancer returns, you pray for peace....or justice and none comes." Afterwards he said he'd had me in mind when he preached the sermon. It was a special sermon and at the end I felt in touch with God. There were tears in my eyes when I talked to Tom. I'm also reminded of the II Cor.4 passage -- we do not lose heart because although our outward nature is wasting away, our inner nature is being renewed day by day. May it be so, God; I do not feel the daily renewal as surely as I did several weeks ago. I feel more in a holding pattern, more distant from God although still beloved, betrothed. I also haven't felt as moved to sing praises, although one song did come to my lips this morning.

I cling to Fay's grace words -- grace to listen, to be open, to entrust myself to God (body and soul); and the grace of gratitude, praise, and joy.

O God, I surrender myself to your love. I will only to will your will. At the same time I would like to live longer, to see my daughter grow up, to hold my husband's hand and know his embrace for years to come. Nevertheless I surrender to your love, your will. As I lift this prayer, I bring with me the pain, the suffering, the tears of so many in the world and even the groaning of the world itself -- ravaged, diseased -- waiting for its redemption along with us. I pray mostly for your Self. I pray also for your shalom to heal us, to wipe the tears away and replace the pain with praise. I praise you now. I think I'm ready for the chemotherapy -- maybe it'll ease the pain in my

38

back, maybe it'll contain and retard the cancer. Nevertheless, I will to will your will for me, O God. I entrust my body and soul to you.

Aug. 20, 1996. Montreat, NC. Had chemotherapy yesterday -- was at the doctor's office 8 hours. I've had very little nausea -- a few brief waves and then I've either drunk some Coke or eaten a peanut butter cracker. My visualization this time has been very different from last time -- last time I could not escape the sense that I was taking in poison. This time the charwomen -- millions of them with wings and head rags -- (the ones from Green Bough) gathered all the Taxol into buckets labeled "hazardous material." Each charwoman has a bucket, and with a pair of tongs, she grabs the dividing cells and shoves them in a slot in the top of the bucket where the Taxol kills my cells. When the bucket is filled, it is closed up and left for disposal and elimination. Then the charwoman goes and gets another bucket. The charwomen are able to climb into the bone's hollow centers and get directly at the cancer cells. These women don't have tongs but a vacuum suction nozzle to suck the cells into the bucket. The most fascinating part of the visualization is that one charwoman has gathered a number of white blood cells into a room in the body where she is retraining them to recognize the cancer cells as an enemy. These cells also return to this room to divide so the charwomen with buckets don't kill them. I've experienced this visualization as very friendly.

A few nights ago I had a very grace-filled experience. I realized that I was (again?) carrying Lucy Mac, Gerry, Dean, and Louie as though they were burdens. It became clear to me that I do not need to carry them; they are not my burdens. My task is to love them every day of my life. But only God carries them and is finally responsible for them. I need to leave them in God's hands -- and love them as best I can. After all, they are, each one, baptized.

We drove up to Montreat today for a few days in Erskine Clarke's cottage. I hope we'll be able to relax and enjoy the mountains and each other.

For almost a week now I've had a new image that replaces my sense of being a fish in the ocean of God's love. Now I am a tiny

39

piece of coral connected to a huge coral reef. God is still the ocean supplying our every need. The sense of being connected to all the other coral is deeply satisfying and comforting. Two other images that continue to sustain me are being a baby in God's womb with my every need supplied by the umbilical cord. In the womb's darkness I feel warm and surrounded by unfailing love, and the other is of being in the anteroom to God's throne room, a gaudy gilt room full of relief curlicues. Often I wait on the floor curled up like a turtle or a scarab and often God draws me into the darkness of the throne room and holds me close -- in a wonderful, wonderful hug or like a mother cradling her baby.

Aug. 25, 1996. Sun. Decatur, GA. We just got home from 5½ days in Montreat, NC. What a restful place to be....and yet I've felt so selfish and petty the last few days, as though Gerry and Lucy Mac were to wait on my every whim and as though every ache or pain were a catastrophe for all to acknowledge. One problem was that I never got into a routine of sitting meditating devotions with Gerry, reading Teresa, and reading Cloister Walk. I did my exercises twice a day after the first day or two. My back hurt too much Tuesday and maybe Wednesday morning. In fact I started taking 45 mg. of MS Contin (morphine) on Wednesday to try to bring the pain down. I'm now down to 15mg. And tomorrow I try switching to Roxicet (codeine). Dr. Peteet indicated that the Taxol should help with the pain if it's working. I hope so.

I realized maybe a week ago that I need to entrust the back exercises to God. If God wants to use them to ease the pain and strengthen my back -- good. But I'm not trying to make anything happen on my own. I want to entrust my body and soul entirely to God and for God's will to be enacted for God's name to be glorified.

Aug. 27, 1996. I've forgotten how to be open. Lucy Mac last night twisted her legs around as I was scratching her back and singing to her. As she twisted, her legs dug into my leg; I fussed at her, unable to be open. Today I've tried to remember my grace words by which

40

I try to live: "Be open." Gerry said he drank the last of "my" caffeine-free Coke. The next bottle was far from cold, having been in the refrigerator maybe 45 minutes. I tried to make a mental adjustment - "I'll use water for my next pills." And I said, "okay." Be open. This afternoon my rectum hurt, after having hard bowel movements for 2 days following five days of constipation. Today my several bowel movements were softer but I was so sore. Ann Connor sent Louie to the store for some medicine. When I went to use the medicine, I knocked the toilet paper roll and the top of the jar of medicine on the floor. I burst into tears, feeling so helpless, knowing how painful it is to kneel down and find the items on the floor. Gerry came in and picked them up. He held me. He also helped put antibacterial cream and a band-aid on a finger I cut yesterday. I cried again, again feeling helpless. It's hard for me to open the medicine drawer because the drawer is big and it sticks. Be open. Be open. Not something I do but a grace I pray for and try to remember throughout the day. Be open -- entrust yourself to God.

Oh God, grant me the grace to be open and to entrust myself to you and grant me the grace of gratitude, praise, and joy.

Aug. 29, 1996. I've cried a lot today. Ostensibly for different reasons. This morning my bottom still hurt so, I cried because of the pain. Then I gathered myself with others in the world in pain and cried to God for the promised shalom when pain, tears, sighing, and death will be no more. For me the promise of shalom is what makes life worth living.

I went to the doctor's office this morning for lab work. The doctor wanted to see Gerry and me. My white cell count was down but within expected limits. I told him of my visualization of the charwomen. We laughed together. It felt good.

This afternoon I cried because I felt so much love for God, not God's love for me but a surge, an overflowing love in me for God. Teresa of Avila doesn't really trust such tears but there was no way for me to stop them and they felt genuine.

Tonight for awhile putting Lucy Mac to bed, I felt very

centered -- in my heart -- or deeper - in the core of my soul. I can't remember Teresa's expression for it (center of the soul, I think). I felt open to God and to the vagaries of life, I felt as though my will was registering zero, as though I simply was able to be and wish for nothing else. It was a pleasant, happy, peaceful experience.

Later while I was doing my back exercises, I found myself crying that Pete Caruthers had died yesterday. He died of brain cancer he's had several years. I cried partly because he's into and through the mystery of death. He knows he's there -- wherever "there" is. I've been praying for him and his family for -- how many years? I can continue to pray for his family, but Pete, where is he? When my brother Tolly died, I was fine. Daddy told us we were crying for ourselves because we'd miss him, but Tolly was with Jesus. Pete is with Jesus, in God's loving presence, in his very own room in the heavenly mansion.

Lucy Mac wrote me a message at school today, addressed to Dr. Lucy A. Rose, 185 Mead Rd. Decatur, GA. 30030. Twenty-five hearts were around this address, mostly pink and yellow, one purple, one orange, one blue. Inside she wrote. "Dear Lucy, I love you. I hope you get well soon. Love. Guess who." She wanted me to guess who sent it. I asked, "Isabel?" She said, "No, it came from school." I said, "The only person I know of at your school who loves me is you." She grinned and said, "Yes."

Aug. 30, 1996. Proofreading Jana's and my manuscript for year C of the *Abingdon Women's Preaching Annual*, I became aware of two ways my sickness has set me apart from the "American Norm." I am desperately aware of how much I am interconnected with and dependent on others -- interconnected through pain and suffering, dependent on prayers and fingers that can type (my back hurts if I sit at the computer very long), and strong arms to lift laundry or move a chair. And secondly, I am no longer desensitized to the pain of the world. Granted I can feel the tug to close in upon my own pain and ignore, even aggressively resist, the link between my pain and the pain of others and the earth. But the Spirit consistently prevents my becoming too self-absorbed. Last night as I reflected on my experience of sharp, prolonged pain yesterday morning, I envisioned the Spirit grabbing me up and throwing me together with the cries and groans and tears of the world's people. And I became briefly, momentarily, these people's priest -- crying out on behalf of us all for God's shalom-presence. Then the Spirit dropped us all into God's lap of love.

Another thought inspired by my proofreading -- I'm moved to reword Luke 1:6-7 (words about Elizabeth). She had committed her life to being righteous before God, to trying to live blamelessly according to all the commandments and regulations of the Lord. But - But - what a "but"... she had cancer that threatened to end her life in midcourse (Ps.102:23-24). This section seems so arrogant somehow. I wish I hadn't written it - as though I'm anywhere near righteous. Ha! But somehow I do feel a kinship with Elizabeth. The words stumble from my lips as the tears well up in my eyes, "O God, I entrust my life, my body, my soul, each day you have determined for me to live to your love. I will only to will your will."

Hallelujah! Songs of praise returned to my lips -- gift songs from the Holy Spirit. In between proofreading I'm also doing laundry. Putting a new load into the washer and folding the load hot out of the dryer, I began to sing "On Eagle's Wings" (a gift yesterday in a card from a Union Theological Seminary classmate, Elaine Rhodes), then "His Eye is on the Sparrow," then "Great Is Thy Faithfulness." How wonderful it was for my heart and my mouth to be singing again -- singing praises, singing of God who can be trusted.

It's 7:00 PM now and I keep crying. I can't see to the source of the tears; I can't remember any trigger -- so different from yesterday's tears. I know I'm tired. I got up at 7:00 AM, got Lucy Mac up for breakfast and we ate our cereal together as usual. I lay back down about 7:45, just before Lucy Mac and Gerry left for school. I slept about another hour and then got up and with Dean's help collected and started the laundry. It turned out to be 4 loads. Then I began reading the manuscript. I ate lunch about 1:00, partly overlapping with Louie, who came in from church having not eaten.

About 1:30, I took the manuscript into the living room so I could watch the first game of a doubleheader with Dean. Around 3:00, I started to fade, to hurt. I should have taken my Roxicets, but I didn't, or I should have lain down and rested my back. Anne Stevens came by at 4:00. I was expecting her and looking forward to her visit. But I was tired and hurting. We talked 2 hours! A wonderful visit! Toward the end we began talking of things that made us both cry -- Lucy Mac, Anne not having a child, so what gets left behind? I told her about Daddy's letter to me. I couldn't tell her without fighting back tears - how most of what he worked for is being changed. To me, what lasts isn't anything tangible, not even Lucy Mac, who could die before me. Maybe it's because of my "thinking like a woman," but to me the legacy one leaves is the differences one's life has made on others, the ways our lives intersect with others and we are catalysts for changes in each other. Anne added, "The hands we held in hospital rooms." "Yeah," I said. Then I shared my unorthodox theology that maybe 1% of Hitler will go to heaven but maybe 90% of Teresa of Avila. Anne laughed. And, I said, where we've helped to up the percentage because of our love or care for someone -- that's our legacy. I write it here sort of dispassionately but I was choking with tears as we talked because -- well, I don't know why. Anne also said something about hating illness; then she said, "I hate the fact that you have cancer." "I know," I answered, "I hate that you have lupus." We held hands for a long time, and with the other hand wiped away the tears. When she left I was <u>very</u> tired....and not through with the tears.

Have I said Anne and I want to write a book out of our experiences of pain? The books I've seen about suffering haven't reflected on it in a way that lets me say, "Yes, that's what I've experienced." We thought today about maybe a chapter that is a book review of a book by someone else, a chapter reflecting on a biblical passage, and a chapter reflecting on a personal experience (the sequence repeated three or four times). I don't know if such a format would work but who knows. She brought me Solle's <u>Suffering</u> and a C.S. Lewis book, plus an article and a sermon. Tonight I read an

44

excellent sermon on suffering by Joan Delaplane. We've got lots of work to do -- maybe it'll get done....and maybe not.

Aug. 31, 1996. Nancy and Mike came to visit today. I didn't go to the airport - Lucy Mac and Gerry went while I slept till 9:10. Actually Peggy's calling woke me. I was glad. The plane came in at 8:41. This morning we played games: Amazing Labyrinth and a kind of Charades with Lucy Mac about the title of 4 books. We went out for lunch and then to Toys-R-Us for a Clue game and a guitar that Nancy and Mike got for Lucy Mac. Then we came back home, tuned the guitar. I took an ibuprofen, and we got the keys and visited the seminary where Nancy and Mike are staying. We got back around 4:30 or 5:00 and from then till 6:00 the three of us sat in the computer room and had a very heartfelt conversation. Around 6:00 Allison brought Lucy Mac back from her afternoon with Jonathan. Whitney came back from a walk with Isabel so we ordered 3 large pizzas from Athens Pizza and the ten of us ate and visited till about 9:00.

During the conversation with Nancy and Mike, I remembered a conversation with Lucy Mac I want to record. Several weeks ago Lucy Mac said, "I don't think we can really know anything about heaven till we get there." "Yes," I answered, "That's why I believe in the Bible to help tell me things I can't otherwise know." Then Lucy Mac said something about God, I think. And I said, "Lucy Mac, God is the most important thing in my life. One reason I can bear being so sick is that I can leave you and Daddy in God's hands." And at some point I said, "Lucy Mac, you realize I may die before most mommies." Lucy Mac said very firmly, "Mommy, this conversation is getting very boring." Needless to say, it ended.

September: I Surrender All

Sept. 1, 1996. Nancy and Mike left tonight before COH worship. This afternoon she and I had another good conversation. She told me about a recent Ursula LeGuin science fiction book in which a man goes to another planet, where he has a nervous breakdown. What

45

saves him is his beginning to sing the songs he remembers from his home planet. Nancy asked me to write down the songs, stories, and activities that are healing and peace-giving for Lucy Mac...and Gerry. I told her the songs I sing to Lucy Mac at bedtime: "Silent Night" and "It Came Upon a Midnight Clear" (first verse of each) and the extra songs I sing to her: all six verses of "Now the Day is Over," one verse of "Oh, Come, Little Children," and three verses of "Away in the Manager." I need to ask Lucy Mac if these later songs are ones that speak to her. [She said, yes.]

Nancy also told me that after a phone conversation with Daddy, he had said "I love you both." She thinks that my illness has allowed the family to express our feelings for each other more vocally. If so, thanks be to God.

It was wonderful having them, and Nancy promised to come back.

Kathleen Murdock called from North Carolina. She is visiting her parents, and asked, "How are you?" as though my attestations that I'm fine wouldn't cut it with her. But I found myself again telling her stories of how my illness has deepened my faith, and how I wouldn't go back to the end of May and pick up there because too many incredible faith-deepening experiences have happened. I then told her about my understanding that for Teresa of Avila, pain and suffering are not evil or the enemy; they can lead to new experiences of God. I think when Kathleen realized that I wasn't fighting but accepting what I was experiencing, she said something that I translated as, "Well, welcome to the rest of the world" [where suffering and loss are the norm]. Then she told me a story of a man in Nicaragua to whom they'd lent money to raise shrimp. He and 7 others had dug 25-acre ground pools. Fish got in one and ate most of the shrimp, but they had the other bed. Then the hurricane destroyed it. He went back to trying to make the shrimp-raising work. Then he had an old Jeep he'd bought from the Sandinistas. The drive shaft -- no, that's not right -- something broke and the Jeep overturned so he broke his back in 6 or 8 places. As soon as possible he was out of the hospital and back trying to get the shrimp business going. Suffering

46

is the norm for the rest of the world, I heard her saying.

Then she told me she prayed for me every time she nursed the baby and she admitted she hadn't prayed in years. She's grateful to me that she's now praying again!

<u>Sept. 2, 1996</u> First a P.S. to the songs Lucy Mac hears from me. Sometimes (not recently too much) she wants me to tell her Daniel and the lions' den, especially when she's afraid. And we sometimes laugh as to whether the angel zipped up the lions' mouths or locked them up or taped them up, and sometimes I say that the King threw all the bad counselors into the den after Daniel was saved and the lions gobbled them up before they even reached the bottom. It's in the Bible. I leave out the part about their wives and children.

Her crying song, to help her through her tears and weepy spells, is ,"Oh, whistle while you work."

Jim, Swami's novice from COH worship, told me Sunday night he'd been meditating and thought of me and the phrase came to his mind, "There is water aplenty." I thanked him, saying I would meditate on the meaning for me. Both last night and tonight I pondered the phrase and realized that my water images -- being in God's womb and being coral in God-the-Ocean -- belonged to my meditation time. I need to carry them to school -- at school where I get so stressed out -- there is water aplenty, amniotic fluid and ocean for us all!

Lucy Mac and I had a wonderful conversation at bedtime about the day -- what was not good, what was. We also prayed for her to find a friend.

<u>Sept. 4, 1996.</u> Wed.   Baptism is about/into a communal way of life at times at odds with secular modes of thought, e.g. "Illness is seen to be as often a way to God as not; death is spoken of in the past tense, and life is all that lies in a future fraught with risks." (Aidan Kavanaugh, <u>The Shape of Baptism: The Rite of Christian Initiation</u>).

A few minutes ago,· while putting Lucy Mac to bed we had another good conversation. As part of it I told her about illness being

47

a way to God. She replied, "Yes, a lot of people die because of illness." "And I might die," I added. "Well," she replied, "Then you will be in a better place." I paused at the truth of her statement and said, "Maybe if I do go to heaven, I will be an angel and can look after you." She responded, "I like the book Someday Heaven, but I think it is wrong about that." "You mean about people not becoming angels?" I asked. "Yes," she answered decisively. She is quite a theologian. I just pray she is also a person of faith in whom convictions about God's love and Jesus' life, death and resurrection, and the hope of heaven are beginning to take root and grow.

Sept. 7, 1996 Sat. Several days ago I had a profound psychosomatic sense that the charwomen were beginning to win the battle with the cancer, that the tide had turned. In my visualizations I imagined the charwomen climbing into the caves and recesses made by the cancer and ferreting out the cancer cells that have created caves and cavities. I envisioned more "dressing-room" type rooms off of every bone cavity and every blood vessel so that the trained white blood cells can divide without the charwomen catching them. The deep sense that maybe I'm going to live has stayed with me. I find myself surrendering to the prayers of those who are praying for my healing, and then I surrender myself to God's will which is pure love for me and for this world which is also longing for shalom.

      Teresa, in the last few chapters about the sixth mansion, has been describing anguish/suffering of the soul as a pulling farther and farther away from the things of this world, a longing for death -- a suffering very different from physical suffering. I have not followed her through these few chapters. With my renewed will to live, which rises from somewhere deep within and floods my body and soul, I find our ways parting. Still she has been a wonderful companion.

Sept. 9, 1996. I cried last night. Gerry held me. Partly because my hair has fallen out, partly because my side hurts -- sore, very sore, to the touch under my left arm -- and partly because Lucy Mac said so plaintively when I put her to bed, "Mommy, I love you," and partly also because I want to live -- to see Lucy Mac grow up, and to move into old age with Gerry. The tears are still lurking just below the surface.

Maybe the parting with Teresa sparked my will to live -- not that I haven't felt it before -- but now it is a very deep feeling. It is not the things of the world that are attractive -- it's Lucy Mac and Gerry; it is even the work I do at Columbia Seminary.

At church yesterday, I spoke and shared my concerns about my ambivalence toward praying with Lucy Mac about the chemotherapy "containing and killing the cancer" (she helped decide on those words). I shared that I know God sometimes says, "No," but how do I help her trust God if God says, "No?" After church Ruth Anne came up to me and said that the prayer Lucy Mac and I prayed encouraged her to change the way she prays. She said, as a life-time Presbyterian, her prayers have always had a kind of fatalism about them -- a kind of God's-will-be-done-because-that's-what-will-happen-anyway prayer. But she has felt encouraged to pray for what she really wants and then leave the outcome to God. I agree with her, but it is risky with a 7-year old. But then I haven't been ending our prayers with, "Your will be done." I need to do that for sure.

While I was at Green Bough, I had an interesting, telling sequence of images that I think worth recording. I had been climbing and climbing a hill. Each time I thought I had reached the top there was more mountain that demanded my ascent. (I was reminded of getting tenure only to find that I had to write an installation address, then the book needed revising for W/JK Press). Finally I realized the mountain would never end -- there is no summit at which I can rest and quit the climb. So, I envisioned myself as having crawled off onto a narrow path that circled the mountain to the right. Once I fell off into space, but God put me back on the mountainside at the beginning of the path. Crawling along I came upon caves hollowed out of the mountainside. I had been told that somewhere along the path was an entrance into the mountain where God is. I decided that the entrance was in the last alcove, so I crawled along the path. Once I rested in an alcove; once I found food and drink in an alcove. I was tired --

tired of climbing and tired of crawling. I realized that **I** had decided that the entrance was in the last alcove; no one had told me that. I sat in the alcove, leaned back, relaxed and fell into the mountain. This visualization/vision repeated itself for several days. Once I found myself back at the beginning of the path on my hands and knees. Without taking any steps, I leaned to my left into the mountain and fell inside. I am so driven by agendas, tasks, goals. I am learning to let God take charge of my life -- No, I am realizing that God is in charge of my life and I am learning to lean into God -- though I am a slow learner.

Sept. 16, 1996. Mon. I am not sure I can sort out the spiritual highs and lows of the last five days. Thursday after my second round of chemotherapy on Tuesday, I began throwing up with a virus. I was miserable, throwing up at first every 20 minutes, then 30, then it slowed in the afternoon when Gerry took me for IV fluids to the doctor's office. I am not a good sick -- I am peevish, moaning now and then over the distress of my stomach, restless -- far from any calmness, peace or centeredness. Gerry said I got frantic a time or two. One of the aggravating problems all day Thursday and Friday was that I could not rest in God, and I found myself singing snippets of songs -- "Woke up this morning found my pillow all gone," "Rescue, rescue aid society" (from "The Rescuers" I watched with Lucy Mac) -- although sometimes I would confuse it with Wheel of Fortune and sing "Rescue, rescue aid society," and lastly a few lines from the theme song of "America's Funniest Home Video", "America, America." They would not get out of my head however hard I would try to sing something else. All I could muster were countless, "Dear God, Dear God, Dear God." I think I found myself really angry at God. I told God this wasn't fair and a few other sentences -- about 2 or 3 in all. It didn't last long. Not long afterwards there began to well up from inside me over and over again, one of two songs, "I surrender, I surrender all. All to thee my precious Savior, I surrender all," or "Count your blessings. Name them one by one. Count your blessings, see what God has done. Count your many

50

them one by one, And it will surprise you what the Lord has done."
And several times I <u>did</u> name my blessings, counting them, lingering
over them, caressing them. What a relief! What grace from an
inscrutable God. I sang them over and over and over.

Sunday morning I watched one sermon and a church service
on TV with Dean. There were a few nice songs in the full service, but
nothing really inspirational for me. The sermons were on why one
should join the church -- pretty didactic, but thoughtful -- and why
one should not worry -- too self-centered for me, but it did lead to a
prayer of recommitment to Jesus Christ which I found meaningful.
The most meaningful part of the morning for me was my reading Job.
It had been helpful when I last had cancer, and I felt moved to read it
through again. Part of what Job says to me is that I am not being
punished -- there is no tit-for-tat that balances this suffering with
previous sins. That is the primary message of all the friends of Job.
I know that, but I found myself choking when I said to Dean, "I am
not being punished." "Of course not," he answered.

Now my take on Job (the way I understand him) is that he
refused that analysis of his (my) situation and the corresponding
understanding of God that accompanies it. And what is so exciting
to me about the book is that he starts off answering the friends and
increasingly begins talking to God. At first it is hard to tell whether
he is addressing the friends or God. Then he says, "If I were to speak
to God, here is what I would say...." Then the next time he says in
effect, "Forget your friends"; and he turns to God as if God were right
there and starts talking. And God does not squash Job for railing, for
questioning, for voicing his doubts and frustrations. In fact, God in
the end says that Job got it right -- he understood God better than his
friends. Maybe not because of Job's content but because he
understood God is a God who wants to be in relationship, in
conversation. For the friends, God was a far-off judge, a tit-for-tatter.
For Job, God was one to talk to, to cling to, to cry to, to plead with.
And God finally says in effect to Job, "You are my beloved. I delight
in you." And maybe if I can cling to God, and cry to God, and bring
my questions and deepest longings to God, God will whisper to me,

51

"You are my beloved and I delight in you."

Even as I write of so many internal, spiritual experiences, I am constantly overwhelmed by the community of the faithful lifting me up, supporting me with prayer and love and cards and calls and kind words. Their love is inseparable from my continuing belief in and my clinging to God's love. I got a card today from the Kingsbridge Retirement Community -- a "thinking of you" card signed by six people I do not know. It was readdressed here from Emory University Hospital -- how did they get my name? How thoughtful!

Sunday afternoon and evening I found myself singing a piece of a song, "For it is Thou, Lord, Thou Lord only, that maketh me to dwell in safety." A welcomed gift from the God of the depths of my soul.

Sept. 18, 1996. Wed. I have prayed that this experience of being sick since Thursday will change me -- not just be something I "got over". And I recognize two consequences for which I am grateful. One is that I have not been able to take any pain medication, and although I have had some back pain, it has been bearable. Today I am better, though my stomach still aches and I am weak, but I do not -- at least now -- feel tempted to try to take/risk some pain medicine.

The other is not a fully articulable insight, yet I will try my best. On Sunday the second preacher commented that in the day of the King James Version of the Bible, to think meant to worry. He pointed out that in the new KJV the translation is "Do not worry," but in the original KJV the translation is "Take no thought for." He then gave two examples from literature in the time of the KJV when thinking meant worrying. One was a play -- something about Cleopatra, I think -- or that was the title -- in which someone says, "Think and die" -- "Worry and die." That got me to wondering about how this equation between worrying and thinking undercuts thinking -- on which our culture places so much importance: thinking is all that seems to matter sometimes (maybe I am reflecting 13 years in an academic environment). And if thinking is not really of ultimate importance, what is its rival or better, its companion?

52

I have not written in this entry in my journal but I did in one about how, through spiritual direction at Green Bough and my "sitting" regularly I "fell into my heart" from my head. I have tried to live out of my head for a long time, when the two really belong together, and for me the heart is more and more a central place in myself for which I live. It is as though I need to let my heart do the thinking, reaching into my mind for information, but bringing it back to my heart for sorting, realizing and deciding. It is important to me that in some languages -- Asian, Hebrew -- the heart is the decision-maker.   So for me, instead of _thinking_ being of primary value, something else is -- whatever the heart does.

During the continuing illness Sunday and Monday, I found myself saying now and then, "I do not understand God," or "This does not make sense." And I realized that is _thinking_ language; I do not _want_ to understand or have it make sense, meaning that I then take that bit of information and live out of it until it needs reworking. Instead I found myself shifting into the heart language of relationship, asking, "How do I live now in relationship with you, God, and with your people, and these people you have given me to live with?" At least one time I found myself centered in my heart. I became aware of a deep center -- maybe Teresa's "center of the soul" or "the deepest depths of the soul" -- where I felt connected to God, where the life I live in Christ fuses with and draws itself from the very life of God. I know I am not articulating this very well, but it is hard to put into language. I also feel very sick.

Today I had another insight into this business of living out of my heart and not my head. I got up this morning after a good night's sleep. I made myself _not_ sleep yesterday, and this morning I felt good. I drank some caffeine-free coke, ate some Rice Krispies with caffeine-free Coke on them and then drank some caffeine-free coke. My body was craving something. Sitting in the rocking chair in the kitchen, I said to myself, "I think I will take a walk today to the railroad tracks and back." The railroad tracks are at the top of the street, past the elementary school, two houses and two big empty spaces -- a long way for someone whose walking distance has been two or three laps

53

from the front door to the back door per day. Then it hit me: I tend to set myself external goals -- walking distance -- walking to the railroad tracks -- that have nothing to do with my internal life/state. I used to do that at Green Bough -- "I am going to walk to the end of the road" -- I never made it. What does it mean to listen internally -- to my body, my spirit? I might say, "I think I will walk outside," but I should not set myself an unreasonable goal. But that is how I have lived my life -- by external goals: paper is due at 5:00, manuscript is due June 6th. Such external demands that have no relationship to my internal needs have dominated my life completely, ruling my schedule, suppressing any sense of an internal rhythm or even inner voices of my body and spirit. So here I am, trying desperately to listen to my body, my stomach. About mid-morning I threw up because my stomach didn't want so much so fast. It is hard to listen with my heart to what my body is saying. I am more used to "finishing what is in the cup," whether my stomach agrees or not. It is 1:20 and for about an hour I have been nursing some Ensure. But I find myself more anxious to "finish the can" than to ask my stomach if it is ready for more. What difference this will all make once I am well, I am not sure. But it seems important -- to listen to my heart internally -- to God, my spirit, to my body, rather than allowing external demands and goals to have <u>sovereign</u> reign. It is their sovereignty, not their importance, that concerns me.

<u>Sept 23, 1996</u>. Green Bough. In all my previous visits here I have come to relax, to unwind. Today I am relaxed, unwound. Occasionally a day will wind me up and I'll feel the old franticness so typical of my living with stress. At such times I'm not centered-in, living from my heart. Usually the next day I've lost most of it. I think Friday wound me up with going to school[1] (sitting up so that the ride hurt my back), listening to a lecture in an old school-desk with an arm

---

[1] Lucy taught regularly at the seminary during the Fall and Spring semesters.

for right-handed note takers (I'm left-handed) (an hour that also hurt my back) and leading or facilitating the discussion in the small group for the second hour. Then I spent two hours at the doctor's office Friday afternoon. Then Saturday a little before 11:00 we (actually Gerry and Dean) put the wheel-chair in the back of the Toyota and with Dean driving, Lucy Mac in the front seat and me lying down in the back seat, we headed for Northlake Mall. There we bought Lucy Mac shoes, long pants, long-sleeved shirts and a clock. Then the three of us ate at a Mellow Mushroom and dropped Lucy Mac off at the movies with Beth Thompson. Dean and I were home a little after 2:00. I didn't unwind from those two days for a long time. Sunday at church I felt sick -- not in pain, but sick in my head and sinuses. I continued to feel bad all afternoon and didn't go to the community worship. By bedtime I had somewhat relaxed back into my heart. This morning I went to school for a 2-hour lecture but I brought a much-more comfortable desk chair from my office to sit in and I put the seat all the way back for the ride over. Then Joy Pruitt picked me up and we came here to Green Bough. I was discombobulated when we got here. Not in my heart, not in touch with my spirit. I lay down to rest my back. I walked outside around the trees, past the flower garden and bird house. I sat in the rocking chair in my room. Finally I went into the chapel. At the door I paused and said, "Holy space, holy space, holy space." I sat down in the chair nearest the statue of Mary and the communion table. Suddenly I relaxed; I was back in my heart. A bird sang, and I longed for all my listening to move me to be open and to entrust myself to God. I yearned for all my seeing and touching and being and doing to issue in gratitude, praise and joy. I realized how everywhere I look in the retreat house there are reminders of the holy. I need that -- I long for that in my home, at school, at Northlake Mall, and the doctor's office. I want to live out of the kind of centeredness in my heart that I have been experiencing lately.

Habakkuk 3:17-19, "Though the fig tree does not blossom, nor fruit be on the vines, the produce of the olive fail and the fields yield no food, the flocks be cut off from the fold and there be no herd in the stalls, yet will I rejoice in the Lord; I will joy in the God of my salvation. God, the Lord, is my strength; he makes my feet like deers' feet; he makes me tread upon the high places."

Like me, Habakkuk faces death from his circumstances if they don't change -- no drink, no oil, no food, no meat. Unlike me, Habakkuk rejoices and exults in God. Yet I can say I will cling to God, or yet by grace will I not abandon my God. But No! Habakkuk rejoices, exults in God and leaps to the heights of the mountains, while I am like one at a banquet, at a huge smorgasbord, or a wedding reception and I pick at the food or settle for a few peanuts and a mint, without ever seeing the sumptuous spread. I know how to rejoice -- there is an echo of these verses in Mary's Magnificat -- "My spirit exults in God, my Savior." Around Lucy Mac's birth I exulted -- was it "in God"? Pregnancy, yes...death, rejoice?

Life is painful because of those who have died.

Joy is painful because of those who weep.

Love is painful because of those who hate.

And while I am living and loving and laughing,

I am waiting for you, O God.

Joy is a grape in a cluster with gratitude and praise.

I fell asleep. I waked and walked around. I went to the bathroom. God whispered, "Joy is down here with peace and love -- you know them. Joy is down here with me!!" My prayer -- "Then lead me, O God, down to you, where facing steady, sure death I can rejoice in you, my God, my Savior, because I am with you."

I was at the banquet, awed by the food. Then I said, "I'd rather be a scarab on the floor in the gilt anteroom waiting for God." A voice said, "You can do both. The door to the banquet is off the anteroom and I can find you in either room."

My back hurts. I'm tense, resisting or trying to make something happen (joy? holy presence?). You've prayed for the grace of rejoicing, wait! Wait restfully, wait watchfully.

I went to the chapel before night prayer and sat in the almost darkness. Tears welled up in my eyes. Why are tears so much closer to my heart than joy? Why is joy so hard to find, to admit? As I sat there I felt a tiny spring begin to seep through from those deepest, darkest depths of my soul. It was ever so minute but like sugar water or purple dye -- enough would make a difference in my whole self.

Steve sang, "In the shadow of thy wings I sing for joy." Oh, God -- give me songs of joy to sing and I will sing them! I promise -- haven't I always sung the songs you have given me?

My back hurts. I cried after night prayer because I was reminded of last time's pain and heartache.

Rejoice in the Lord always and again I say rejoice.

Rejoice ye pure in heart

Why should I feel discouraged...

I sing because I'm happy...

Joy is like the rain.

Fay helped me recognize my spats of anger lately and to legitimate them. In four months my life has been deeply disrupted. When I feel anger or fear, I need to let myself experience the emotion deeply and move through it into the arms of God. Last Friday taking a shower -- naked and wet -- I discovered there was no soap in the soap dish. Muttering accusations against the last person to decimate the soap and leave the soap holder empty, I turned off the water, half-dried my feet (a hard, sometimes painful task), slid them into my slippers, wrapped my bathrobe around me and dripped out to the linen closet. All this took considerable time. On the way out of the bathroom, I threw open the bathroom door with a bang and threw open the linen closet door with another bang. Then I discovered there was no soap in the linen closet. I yelled, "No soap. There is not even any soap in the closet." I was hysterical and crying. Gerry came and made me sit down. He asked gently why I was so upset. I think three and a half months of cancer and ten days of a stomach virus had left me vulnerable. Surely a few things can go right -- like expecting soap in the shower soap holder. I was embarrassed but I was also venting my frustration at life's being turned upside down in such a short time. Yesterday I got through class at 10 minutes to one. Gerry had said for me to call. I called -- busy! To call I have to stand up because the phone is too far from any of the chairs in my office. I called again, and again -- busy! I got more and more frustrated -- again life wasn't going my way on my schedule. On top of that I had had a headache off and on Saturday, Sunday and Monday. Dr. Peteet had said that a headache can be a sign the cancer has spread to my brain. Finally after one more busy signal, I sat down in a chair and started to cry just as Gerry came into the office to take me home. He was downloading a big file from Emory. Then yesterday the ride down here wasn't easy. My back and neck hurt. Dr. Peteet had asked me specifically if I had had pain in those two places. I was afraid the cancer was active there, destroying the bones. I realize today I was angry at the pain. Even this morning after the pain medication last evening, my upper right back and neck were still sore. But pain medication this morning eased it, and now early afternoon there is no recurrence of the pain there. The issue is recognizing, valuing and moving through my anger and fear. Fay said, "Be open to your anger and fear," just as I try to be open to God, to the bird's song, to my tears and to the experiences of resting in God's love. Be open to the fear and anger that the chemotherapy may not work or may not work for long, that my life has been violently disrupted by the cancer and the viral attacks. And Fay said for me to remember the deep place within where I am held in the arms of God, in the "dazzling darkness," or where I rest, totally taken care of in God's womb. "Be gentle with yourself," she said.

Dr. Peteet called my ten days of being sick -- and off all pain medication -- a "blessing." He said the lack of pain medication and my not needing any are the best indicators that the chemotherapy may be working.

I have had such an odd series of experiences and insights. I don't know if I can do them justice. I woke from a short afternoon nap around 4:15. Eucharist is at 4:30. I roused myself and went into the chapel early to be in that silent, holy space. Just as Fay and Steve came in I began to notice my back was uncomfortable. The thought of running and taking a pain pill flashed through my mind but I didn't entertain it for a moment. Eucharist is a serious ritual here. I had been asked to read the Gospel and did so. Walking to the lectern and reading a short passage standing did not bother me. But sitting in the silence that followed the readings, I felt the pain inch up the scale. By the time we were standing around the table waiting for the bread and wine, my back was throbbing with pain. I began to understand Paul's words about participating in the suffering of Christ. Surely his back and so much more of him ached and hurt on the cross. I was experiencing during the sharing of the bread and wine something of what Jesus suffered. That insight did not ease the pain but it made the pain bearable, and it intrigues me. After Eucharist I came back to my room, took a pain pill and lay down for it to take effect (or not, in which case I would take another one). Lying here I again thought of Jesus on the cross, his hands ripping against the nails, his shoulders and neck muscles stretched and bent in contorted patterns. So much pain racing through him. My only comparable experience of ever increasing pain was childbirth. But then I knew I was bringing a child into the world. I anticipated joy and life on the other side of my pain. Suddenly my mind switched back to Jesus. He was dying -- but it was as though a light bulb went on in my understanding -- Jesus knew he was bringing forth eternal life, he was birthing salvation into the world. And maybe my pain is the birth-pangs of new life in Jesus Christ, in me and in others who give praise to God because of me and my experiences.

The O.T. readings today at Eucharist were from Proverbs and Psalm 119. It occurred to me that the way of God or following God's righteous way is not a matter of figuring out covenant principles or following divine laws that are obvious and never-changing, but it is a matter of following the path God opens before us moment by moment. It is like following Jesus, who is not a set of directions or a map but a person, and my responsibility is, by grace, to discern where Jesus is leading me moment by moment.

Jesus, Thou Joy of loving hearts,
Thou fount of life, Thou life of all.
From the best bliss that earth imparts
I turn unfilled to heed thy call.

Sept. 24, 1996 John 1:35-39. What are you looking for? I was cool, calm: health and healing. Why? So I can keep on being Lucy Mac's mommy and Gerry's beloved, and so I can glorify God's name.

What are you looking for? I was close to tears: a place to cry out my hurt and fear and the turmoil of the last four months. Jesus sat down and held me as I cried.

What are you looking for? I was listening to the bird's exultant song. A new way of life, a way of living more faithfully. "Follow me." I don't know you very well, Jesus. I know about you. I've read the Gospels over any number of times. But I don't know you very well. He smiled at me, "Follow me."

Isaiah 24:4-10. So bleak -- tears well up -- should I say with Habakkuk: Yet I will rejoice in God? Be still. And in the stillness Jesus said, "Follow me." He took me into the world of Isaiah 24. I saw a family, heads bowed for the blessing. The meal was very meager. I saw a small boy kneeling by his bed saying his prayers, counting his day's blessings. And Jesus showed me an old man, bending to pick up an old musical instrument that sounded to me like a guitar. He tuned it and began to pluck it. The older village kids drew around. Then he began to sing of the past, and of God's promised future and of the God of the Covenant who is faithful.

-And me, Jesus, what about me?

-What are you looking for?

-A new way of living more faithfully.

-The corners. Remember the corners are more important than the center. The corners of a room, a city, a nation. The prophets often came from border towns. You can't see as clearly from the middle.

-So what does this mean for my cancer?

-Don't look at it head on. Find a corner from which to view it. Find corners. In the corners of the world the situation Isaiah describes is reality -- the bleakness, the certain steady advance of death. Yes, you belong there but joy is first a gift to the one rejoicing. Manufactured "joy" is heartless and cruel. Forced "joy" is insincere and destructive. But God-connected joy is deep-rooted in a people's memory and hope; such joy is healing and contagious.

Wade gave me several cacti, one of which was blooming. He said, "The cactus blooms even in the desert."

O God, may my joy bloom even when the vines wither and the fields lie empty and I can hear the steady advancing feet of the angels coming for to carry me home. May I remember that death lies in the past -- in my baptism -- and ahead is only life fraught with risks. To live the life I live in Jesus Christ -- therein is joy and peace.

Wait a minute. I read Isaiah 24:4-10! Let me go to Isaiah 25:4-10! What a contrast! Any joy now in this life is a faint reflection of the joy on the day of salvation when the God for whom we have waited is present in fullness and holiness.

First, God the refuge and shelter -- the God I have experienced in my recent times of pain and fear. Then God the feast-giver and destroyer-of-death who wipes away our tears -- the God of the future for which I long and for whom I pray in my pain. And finally God recognized in fullness because we have already known God in our waiting here. My most terrifying "vision" was my looking down from heaven and seeing Lucy Mac and Gerry miserable and homeless on the streets. And I ran to God and began beating with all my might on God's chest shouting and crying, "You deceived me. You're not the God you said you were. You lied. You lied. You lied." But here the people are filled with joy because who God really is, is the God they'd believed in and bet their lives on. How deeply satisfying.

I imagine I'm in heaven, and someone I know says, "Lucy, this is God." And I look deeply into God's eyes -- all the way to God's heart. And I respond, "Yes, of course. So you're God. I thought so."

To recognize God -- what a profoundly satisfying, joy-filled experience.

And my hope is to begin to recognize God here -- day after day, hour after hour, minute after minute -- because only then -- if I wait on God here -- will I recognize God in heaven.

And Jesus says, "Follow me. No one knows the Father but the son." I sigh. "How about daughters and mothers?" Jesus didn't answer.

Ephesians 1:17-23. Paul prays that God will give the

61

Ephesians the spirit of wisdom and revelation as they come to know him; so that, with the eyes of the heart enlightened, they may come to know hope, the riches of the inheritance of the saints and the greatness of God's power. The sentence runs from verse 15 to verse 23. (Insights from the Greek-English interlinear:)

- The prayer is that God may give them a spirit of <u>sophia</u> and <u>revelation</u> in (en) a <u>full</u> knowledge (epignosei) <u>of him</u> (autou), having been enlightened the eyes of the heart of you for (eis) your knowing (to' eidevai = know into) what is the hope of the calling (kleseos), what the riches of the glory (doxos) of the inheritance <u>of him</u> in (en) the saints, and what the excelling greatness of the power <u>of him</u> toward (eis = into) us, the believing ones, according to the operation of the might of the strength of him, which he has operated in Christ raising him from dead and seating him on God's own right hand. It is the heart that is enlightened by the spirit of wisdom and revelation that knows these mysteries. So pray for a spirit of wisdom and revelation -- it is <u>that</u> which will enlighten my heart to know hope, my inheritance, and God's power.

But I already know these things vaguely. But what is intriguing is the chain: God to my new spirit, my new spirit to my heart. Do I need to reverse the chain -- speaking to my heart to speak to my spirit to speak to God? Not really. I can <u>speak</u> directly to God but I wonder if the telephone wires aren't the spirit and the telephone my heart: Weird!

Still -- what is a spirit of wisdom and revelation? Revelation (apokalupheos) -- the last book in the Bible (Apokaluphis Ioannou = Revelation of John) or a revelation of Jesus Christ that God gave to him (1:1a). Is a spirit of revelation a spirit open to Jesus Christ, to God's spirit? Is it a spirit that can discern the things of God that are necessary and communicate them to my heart? If so, then, dear God, please give me a spirit of revelation. I have in the past asked for wisdom and it's not that I think I'm wise. But with wisdom I thought I understood. I forgot that wisdom is momentarily given, a gift of the moment. And even when I remembered, I was focused on doing, not on the giver of the gift. With revelation the gift is clearly spontaneous and related only to the moment. With revelation surely I would not be inclined to ignore the giver, but in fact the relationship with the giver would be more important than the gift. Oh God, please, grant me a spirit of revelation -- or, is this a corporate gift? Oh well, I can still pray.

The other part of this passage that strikes me is the heaping up of praise to God. I don't live so that a daily utterance of praise issues from my lips. Now and then I sing "Sing God a simple song, laude, laude. Make it up as you go along for God loves all simple things. And God is the simplest of all." I am ashamed. Every morning I should begin the day with praise -- a hymn -- a prayer. Dear God, I am so self-centered. I take your creation, your preserving me through the night, your awakening me to a new day for granted. Forgive me my silent heart, my sealed lips. Give me songs of praise and joy each day. Fill my heart with thanksgiving and praise. May the spirit of revelation open the eyes of my heart that I may recognize your handiwork new every morning and open my lips to express the overflowing of my heart.

Maybe the spirit of revelation recognizes the Jesus who says each morning, "Follow me." Follow me one more day, follow me through the twists and turns, the temptations, the pain, the satisfactions of this day. Please, God, grant me a spirit of revelation that I may praise you and follow Jesus every day.

I'm singing again! Oh joy! Rejoice the Lord is king! Joy to the world. Jesus thou joy of loving hearts. Gloria, gloria in excelsis deo; Gloria, gloria, alleluia, alleluia. And the chorus to "Angels We Have Heard on High" = Glo-o-o-o-o-o-o-r-ia in excelsis deo.

Now that I am living in my heart with some regularity, I am amazed at what a fortress it is -- how walled up and shut-off from connections that are important.

Fay gave as a passage Eph. 1:17-23. My meditating on those verses led me to pray for a spirit of revelation. It seems to me the spirit of wisdom, or the wisdom dimension of the spirit, moves between the heart and the head. I've prayed for wisdom (as James invites us to do) and -- it is not that I think I am wise -- but I at least have a glimpse of what wisdom is. But what is a spirit of revelation? If the spirit of wisdom moved up and down from heart to head and back, perhaps the spirit of revelation moves from the heart deeper into the soul's depths where one's new life flows into and out of God. Perhaps the spirit of revelation could keep me more daily, more hourly, more moment by moment in touch with and aware of God. So I prayed for a spirit of revelation. Tonight before night prayer, I went early into the chapel. Before entering I said, "Holy space, holy space, holy space, and holy is the one entering to meet the Holy One who is everywhere." I went in and sat down. It was then that I realized how shut up my heart has been. According to Ephesians 1:18 the spirit of wisdom and revelation opens or enlightens the eyes of the heart. I prayed that the eyes of my heart situated on the Godward inner side might be open and the heart's ears too. Then -- and I am sure this was prompted by our renovating the kitchen at home -- adding two big windows into the backyard -- I had the image of unshuttering a house to reveal a big picture window and then removing the glass from the picture window and taking the hinges off the door and removing the door. I want my heart open -- wide open -- to the God-direction of my being, to the deepest depths of my soul. I found myself ashamed, sitting in the chapel darkness, deeply ashamed that during my wrestling spiritually with the cancer and during the illness caused by the virus I had at times touched God or been touched by God and then I must have retreated to my boarded-up heart and wondered where God was. I felt a profound sense of shame that I faced, acknowledged, confessed and repented of. Now I hope the channels into the inner recess of myself are as open and uncluttered as the channels to my head where I used to live and to which I used to return as easily as though I were a helium balloon. Staying in my heart used to be so hard. One of the blessings of the wrestling of this past four months is that I am now more securely situated, centered in my heart, more because I lose the center far too often.

My shame was also because I realized how little I praise God. How seldom I voice my gratitude for God's goodness and steadfast love.

Sept. 25, 1996. Fay and I had a good session of spiritual direction. I read to her sections of my notes and two sections above about the dismantling of my boarded up heart and my experience at Eucharist. We agreed that I should do some kind of morning prayer -- keep a hymnbook handy and sing a hymn of praise and repeat a psalm that I've memorized. I want to do that. Also she reminded me of the practice I had not remembered this side of my last viral illness -- whenever I am aware of not being in touch with God, I am to pray a repetitive prayer. I think I'll pray, "I open myself to you, O God." The word open has layers of meaning -- the unboarded heart open in a Godward direction, and its partners as a grace word: "listen" on one side and "entrust yourself to God" on the other.

Fay said a remarkable thing about entrusting myself to God. She said that God is entrusting God's self to me -- that is a part of my experience at Eucharist with pain. She said, "Open yourself to that." I replied "I can't not." She later said, "Take very seriously what came to you with Jesus." I will; I'll ponder its meaning while I am here.

Fay also said, "Your suffering affects the whole universe." I have a lot to learn.

I want to go back to the insight that God entrusts God's self to me. I have been aware of how the Bible speaks of everything we give to God coming to us -- or coming to us first and we then give to God. I first became aware of this with the word worship -- worthship. We give worth to God and God gives worth to us. For me, being "worthed" is the most necessary experience for me to have -- and I cannot find my worth in work or relationships, or things get all distorted. So God worths me and I worth God. A medieval song went: So God is comen to worship us. Yes! And we worship God. We bless God and God blesses us -- although the order is reversed -- God is the first blesser. We glorify God, God glorifies us. We sanctify God, God sanctifies us (Heb. 2:11). We entrust ourselves to God, God entrusts Godself to us -- got to ponder that one in my heart.

Hebrews 2:9-18 (Specially verse 10 which reads, "For it was fitting that he, for whom and by whom all things exist, in bringing many sons to glory, should make the pioneer of their salvation perfect

65

through suffering.") What strikes me is that the suffering of Jesus is meaningful, intentional -- his going through suffering results in his being crowned with glory and honor, his becoming perfect and leading many to glory and honor, his destroying the might of the devil -- the fear of death that enslaves many people, his being able to help those who are tempted. If (or as) I participate in the sufferings of Christ, I pray that I may experience suffering that is meaningful, that results in my being able to help others and in God's using me to lead others to glory. If that is the case, then what I have been through will have been worthwhile. I know my own faith is deeper and I hope stronger because of these last 4 months.

This is a rich passage. I will need to come back to it again and again.

God is the One out of whom all comes, including Jesus and us (v. 11). I don't like the NRSV. The wording we "all have one Father" eliminates the touch of mysticism that is in the Greek. The KJV reads, "For both he that sanctifieth and they who are sanctified are all of one." The Greek ends "out of one all" (ex enos pantes). Now clearly Jesus is crowned with glory and honor, but Jesus is also on our level -- calling us siblings (adelphos) and children (paidia) and being a help when we are tested/tempted because "he himself was tested by what he suffered." I like the NRSV here -- Greek, "has suffered he being tempted, becoming like us so that he can be our high priest, merciful and faithful, before God."

The word "perfect" is teleiosai = to be at one's telos, i.e. one's intended end point of growth. I don't see how suffering could make one perfect in some abstract sense, but to participate in the sufferings of Christ -- if that embraces others, or is on their account, it might make me more what God has in mind for me to be. I love v. 12 in the Greek: en meso ekklesias humneso = in the midst of the called-out (i.e. the church) I will hymn thee. That needs to be my affirmation: I will hymn God every day! I am struck by v. 15, "And free those who all their lives were held in slavery by the fear of death" (NRSV). I've seen and felt that fear in many people since the reemergence of my cancer. I am a reminder that life doesn't always go according to plan

66

-- the plan being that death is delayed till one's 70s or 80s. To face death in one's late 40s isn't the life-plan. It shakes some people's understanding of God so that God's only "faithful" action is a miracle of total healing. That's okay -- I pray for healing. But God may just have other plans for me. My prayer is that I be open to God and to what God is doing with, through and for me.

I want to come back to this -- "We see Jesus." I've been focused on the female to the exclusion of the male. I've been focused on darkness as good to the exclusion of light. Fay said this morning: There is a place where all divisions are one in the depths of God. All out of One: male-female, black-white, darkness-light.

(Here I walked the short circuit all the way!)

More odd experiences that seem inarticulable, especially when I so quickly forget the words I have said or the thought. At lunch today I looked at the plate -- so colorful and filled with good things to eat -- that I immediately thought, "O taste and see that the Lord is good." As I bowed my head for a silent blessing, I said something like, "O God, I know I am not really eating you but in a way I am. You are the life that is in this food; you fill all things; I am thankful for you, O God. Gloria, Gloria in excelsis deo." Then as I ate and I thought -- life is always sacrificing for life. That is what the food chain is. There can be no life if life is not sacrificed. So I thanked each food on my plate for its giving its life that my life might continue -- the strawberries, the grapes, the tuna (I envisioned it deep in the sea), the lettuce, the nuts. And I was deeply aware that by my life's partaking of their life we are one -- as I am one with all life and all creation. A bird's song pushed its way among my thoughts and I remembered that yesterday I was a bit envious of the bird's ability to sing so exuberantly. I wanted to be able to sing praises so full-bodiedly. At the lunch table I realized the bird was singing for me, singing my song on my behalf. And I could lift up the bird's song to heaven as my song of praise. We are not two -- the bird and I -- we are one. As two we need two songs of praise -- two throats and mouths. As one we share a song, the one singing what I, without trill and chirp and inner music, cannot sing except in my heart. So my

67

heart joined the bird's and sang praises to our God who is so good. Somewhere in this inner chain of thoughts I realized that if I must sacrifice my life sooner than I would like, my prayer is that the lives of others are not diminished but enriched, nourished, fed deeply and wholesomely by the life I have lived.

Colossians 1:24-27. Another rich passage. Three parts struck me. (1) Paul's description of his suffering in the flesh on behalf of Christ's body, the church, in order to fill up what is lacking in Christ's afflictions. (2) The mystery now revealed is Christ in you, the nations or Gentiles. And (3) Paul's desire to present everyone mature (perfect) in Christ. If Jesus Christ was made perfect through his sufferings, the Gentiles are made perfect (are brought to their intended end) through Paul's suffering. So why do I suffer if my sufferings are not in vain and useless, which they are not, because I already believe that through them I am participating in the sufferings of Christ. But, am I simply participating in them -- they being the real thing, mine a reflection (one the antitype, one the type, I forget which is which). Or are my sufferings extending Christ's sufferings into 1996 in a way that couldn't otherwise be accomplished? Are my sufferings allowing God's salvation to be birthed in the world in 1996 in a way that participates in Christ's suffering but that could not happen because Christ's sufferings are somehow not complete without Paul's, mine and the sufferings of others -- and, is it all others, or is it only those whom God especially chooses and calls and equips for the task? I don't know the answer to all these questions. And I'm not sure I want to think about what I am experiencing in such a way -- it seems too grandiose. I think I'll return to my prayer: O God, grant me the grace to be open to you.

The second two phrases belong together: Christ in us -- us brought to our telos in Christ. Christ in us -- the life we live Godwardly, the life that doesn't die but lives in the seed planted in the ground and is resurrected into a new body, the life that begins in baptism when the worldly self begins to die and the holy saintly self (Col. 1:26) begins to live -- that life is Christ's; participates in Christ; merges, mingles, mixes with Christ; flows into and out of Christ; and that life has a telos which the diakonos (Col. 1:25) = ministers/deacons of the church nurture. Because the life is in Christ, the telos is in Christ; but turned this second direction I am aware of the communal dimension of this second use of Christ, whose body is the called-out-ones, the church (v. 24). If Christ is in us both as a community and as individuals, our individual and communal teloi are in Christ -- a communal, conglomerate, all-embracing One. So that our destinies, the fulfilment of our individual natures -- these are inseparable from the whole, from our together being church, saints, the in-Christ-ones.

O Jesus, I have promised to serve thee to the end.
Be thou forever near me, my Master and my friend.
I shall not fear the battle if thou are by my side
Nor wander from the pathway if thou wilt be my guide.

At Eucharist today I took the broken piece of bread and I held it and ate it. It is Christ's broken body, symbol of his suffering. And the words came into my consciousness, "O Jesus, I covenant to participate in your sufferings as you call me to share them with you. I covenant by grace to follow you."

It's after supper now and my account of this afternoon's Eucharist is highly abbreviated. I don't know if I am embarrassed or miffed or what. Two other things happened as well. At some point I realized I wasn't centered in my heart. I prayed that God would help me center in my heart. Prayer time came. Steve prayed. Joy prayed. Fay prayed. I don't think I have ever prayed out loud in all the times I've been coming to Green Bough. This time I said to God, "If you have anything you want me to say, I'll say it." Next thing I knew I was praying, choking and stumbling over the words. I prayed for those who cry out, who don't even know God but who cry out in grief and torture and pain. And I prayed for God's shalom, when God wipes away tears and death is no more. I could not believe I was praying and so close to crying. The second experience was that Fay has lent me an orthopedic pillow for sitting -- I took it into the chapel because we sit for a long time during the Eucharist. Today Fay decided we'd stand around the table for the eucharistic prayer. Well,

69

I always say, I lie better than I stand. But my back wasn't hurting too bad, so I took my place in the half circle of four. Even when I am not hurting the eucharistic prayer to me is long -- though meaningful if read -- prayed! -- well. Nevertheless with each new description of God's mighty acts the pain turned up a notch. The prayer ended; the pain was raging just as Steve took the bread and broke it. I can see it in his hands; I watch it break. We began to say, "Lamb of God, you take away the sins of the world, have mercy on us." Once. twice. "Grant us peace." Pain -- participation in the suffering of Christ -- eucharistic bread -- broken body -- pain. At this point, as is typical at Green Bough, Steve said "This is the Lamb of God who takes away the sin of the world. Happy are we who are called to this table." And we responded, "Lord, I am not worthy to receive you, but only say the word and I shall be healed." One, my mind flashed to Psalm 46:6, "God uttered his voice, the earth melted" -- "The word that can cause the earth....the cancer....the pain to melt -- say the word, God." I thought. And two, the pain vanished. Add at this point, tears welling up in my eyes, my covenantal words to Jesus, "O God, give me grace to be open to my own unanticipated don't-have-a-place-for experiences."

Philippians 3:10-14, 20-4:7. Oh, these are good words. And the Greek (which I read in the interlinear!) is so layered for me in meaning.

V. 10. Paul yearns "to know him (Christ Jesus) and the power of his resurrection and the fellowship (koinonia) of his suffering. I long to know Christ Jesus and the other too if Jesus so desires.

V. 12. Then Paul claims that he has not been perfected, brought to completion or to his telos.

V. 13. Nor has he laid hold, though in v. 12 he has been laid hold of by Christ.

So far I'm with him. I've been laid hold of but I can't yet grasp that for which I yearn -- shalom, full life in Jesus Christ -- but that is where my telos -- my fulfilment or completion is moving me. And I'm beginning to glimpse the meaning of a kononia of suffering with Christ -- just a glimpse.

70

And I love Paul's language: Our citizenship is in heaven. Yes, certainly not here, though I benefit from my U.S. citizenship daily and live in uneasy tension with it. And I'm waiting for the change from this body of humiliation and decay and rot and pain to a body of glory! To believe in the riches that await us on the other side of the door called death is to see the poverty of this world's wealth. I believe Benedict's watchword: Keep death daily before your eyes. I also believe I would profit from keeping before my eyes the glory of the riches of our inheritance among the saints (Eph. 1:18) that comes to us fully in heaven. And here? They are present in God's gifts -- God's grace gifts of joy (4:4), peace (4:7), hope (Eph. 1:18), praise.

I had an odd "conversation" with "God" in the chapel after night-prayer tonight. It was as though God said, "You give me praise every morning and I'll give you Jesus to follow." I almost laughed out loud. "No, God, you're not really saying this." "Uh-huh, I am." "So, no praise, no Jesus?" "No, I'm not saying that. But I will say you might miss him, might not recognize him that day." "Oh." There was a long pause. I broke the silence. "Okay, I'll try but you'll have to help me." "Of course."

My back began to hurt during night-prayer and I'd taken a pain pill 40 minutes beforehand. It should have been beginning to take effect, and the pain had just been an ache when I had taken the pill. Then, after my conversation with God, I realized how tense my back was. I tried to relax the muscles; the pain eased a bit, I relaxed more and more, until the pain slipped away. Wow! How tense I am so much of the time. I hope my learning to live with an open heart means my letting go of the tension, the stress, that creeps into my back, coils itself around my bones and the fibers of my muscles, and squeezes tight -- then tighter -- then even tighter.

I found myself ending my prayers tonight with, "And, dear God, please give me a song of praise in the morning so that I may recognize and follow Jesus." I was smiling, remembering the funnyish conversation I had had with God. And I prayed further, "God, you are so wonderful. I came here with no memory of joy, and you have restored my soul to joy and praise. I feel as though I am starting a new chapter in this journal or this journey is something about Jesus and me, because this new chapter is about my being in the world -- and Jesus knows the world! Or maybe, just maybe, this is the beginning of a new fairy tale.

October: His Eye Is On The Sparrow

Oct. 1, 1996. It has been 6 days since I have written anything. And I've been in a lot of pain from my neck. When I wake up in the morning, I can't move it any direction more than an inch without pain shooting through my neck like fireworks. Both in the morning and at night, and at any other time I lay my head down, I have to support my head directly above my body or the pain is excruciating. I don't know if I wrote in my Green Bough notes that I woke up with this Thursday morning of last week at Green Bough.   Friday I went to school for the 2-hour class[1]. My small group did a great presentation. I made a comment at the board at the end of class. It was worth going, and the chair I sat in that had been placed in the corner of the room for me wasn't bad, although it is not as good for my back and neck as my tiltable desk chair.

Sunday I did not go to church because of my neck but I did go to COH worship in the evening. The reflection was about talking honestly to God. Two women responded that they sometimes go to God for a visit, but then almost immediately run away mentally to take care of the thoughts that flood into their minds. I began to feel ashamed that I get so discouraged about the neck pain and want it desperately to go away. When I am in pain, I talk to God, I cling to God as my only hope, I pray for the pain of the world's people and the earth. When I am not in pain I pursue my own agenda and tend to forget about God for long periods of time. I thought: maybe God wants me to learn to live more intentionally aware of God's presence,

---

[1] Lucy continued to teach classes in preaching and worship at Columbia Seminary during the Fall.

a presence I have to practice and practice and practice -- before I return to a faster speed because now I tend to forget God's abiding presence.

Last night when Gerry and I began our together time, I started crying, and I couldn't quit crying. No particularly evident cause surfaced. Gerry prayed a wonderful prayer for us. Then today, when I went to my 3rd round of chemotherapy, Dr. Peteet said the X-rays indicated there has been bone deterioration while I've been on the Taxol. His conclusion was that the Taxol was not working. So he shifted me to another chemotherapy -- Navelbine. I was very discouraged. (Taking my shower this morning I found myself singing, "Why should I feel discouraged...His eye is on the sparrow, and I know he watches me.") Here I was discouraged, but I think I cried most of the tears out last night. A few tears formed in the corners of my eyes off and on for the next 4 hours I was in the office, but I didn't cry on the X-ray table as I had earlier for the first time. Dr. Peteet shifted me to chemotherapy. If this doesn't retard the cancer, all that is left are Crytoxan and Adriamycin that I took 3 years ago and both made me very nauseated. I am beginning to feel hopeless about living. When I first found out about the bone cancer, I felt certain I would die in a fairly short time -- 6 months to a few years, but 1½ years is the average and I sort of anticipated that. But on the Taxol I had a clear sense that the charwomen were winning, and I very much began to want to live a long time. Now the hopelessness is about returning to face the possibility of imminent death. Hopelessness is probably too strong a word -- but the internal shift seems very dramatic. Maybe the Navelbine will work, but I tried to visualize the charwomen: there were not many inside and they were using this chemotherapy differently -- spraying it in the bone cavities formed by the cancer and hollows in the bone centers and collecting it in the buckets. I know God loves me and my family, and I know God will never, never abandon me -- if God abandoned Jesus on the cross, it was so that Jesus as God would experience what we would never have to experience. Or, if I feel abandoned, God is carrying me or letting me

73

share a partnership (koinonia) in Jesus' suffering so that others will give glory to God. I do not seek fellowship in Jesus' sufferings, but I will welcome it -- okay, accept it -- if such partnership comes. Teresa of Avila describes a weaning from the things of this world and an ever-increasing love for the divine Beloved until one yearns for death and union with the divine Spouse with all one's spirit. Maybe, if I do need to shift to a mode that faces death (or the losing of earthly life) since true death is behind me in my baptism and the life and love in Christ is being renewed and strengthened toward eternal life), I will revisit the last two mansions in Teresa's Interior Castle and let her guide me again. In the meantime, I think I will keep trying daily to have a morning time in which I praise God. I will keep entrusting myself to God and praying for the grace to be open, I will keep trying to live out of my heart, and I will try to "keep death daily before (my) eyes" as Benedict advises.

There is another story I want to record. Dr. Peteet ordered a series of X-rays as a base-line to see if the Navelbine is working or not. I've a warm conversational relationship with the X-ray technician, so when I lay down on the table, he asked how I was. I told him, not so good since Dr. Peteet had determined that the chemotherapy was not working and had switched me. I think I told him I was discouraged. He then asked me if I'd seen a movie on TV over the weekend with Farrah Fawcett in it. I said, "No." He summarized the plot -- Farrah, the mother, had shot her 3 kids (apparently this happened several years before Susan Smith drowned her kids.) One child died, one was completely paralyzed, one couldn't talk. The big, question was: who had shot the children? Not until the 3rd child regained her speech and indicated the mother had shot them did the mystery come to light. The X-ray technician confided he couldn't get the story or the images out of his mind. I said, "Stories like that can tap into deep stuff and demand to be dealt with." The technician was in and out of the office space -- turning on the X-ray machine, repositioning me. After I responded, the next time he came back to the table where I was lying, he said, "My mother shot herself in front of me when I was little." "Oh," I said. "Wow. No wonder the movie

74

was so powerful. Did she kill herself?" "Yes, but I was only two. I don't remember it." But memories like that don't go away. They lie deep, waiting to be worked through. We said a few more things and then he shifted to another topic. As I was leaving I told him I hoped he could process the movie adequately. He stared at me hard and said, "I'm reading a book about adult children dealing with memories about their parents." "Good," I said. "Do you believe in prayer?" "Oh, yes," he answered and added something that reinforced his Yes. "I'll pray for you. Okay?" I asked. He either nodded or said Yes with a deep smile that seemed to say he'd been touched. I thought later if he opened up a little because I shared my disappointment at the shift in chemotherapy, I'm thankful to be able to be present to someone else in his pain. And I hope my prayers profit him as he processes the movie and his memories that he can't remember.

I got to thinking about the presence of God while sitting at the doctor's with the IV running. At this time in my life there is an "introverted" sense of God's presence that is a sense of connectedness -- true connectedness -- because the life I live toward God is Christ. (Paul is my mentor here -- and Teresa). And there is an "extroverted" sense of God's presence that I am not good at practicing at all. That is the Jesus from Green Bough I am just beginning to live with in the world.

After Gerry and I had talked to the doctor and he had left us in the room, we hugged and I choked, "And I wanted to be all right." Gerry said, "You will be all right, even if you don't live." He is right, so right. Once when I told Lucy Mac I might die, she answered, "Then you'd be better off." Yesterday she came home with a list of family tree members on my side: Lucy Atkinson McIlwaine, Mama and Aunt Alice, me, Nancy, Peggy, B, Tolly, and the twins (the last three are in heaven), her and Isabel. Interesting she included Tolly and the twins.

Sunday, Oct. 13, 1996. 5:00. I haven't written in a long time. I've been down and okay and down again. The chemotherapy I think has been making me a bit nauseated almost every day since last Tuesday. But I think the real reason I have not written is that I have been fighting internally -- way below consciousness -- to come to terms with the fact that the Taxol did not work. I was beginning to bet on "life." Finally I think I have arrived at a 50-50 place -- 50% betting on living, 50% okay about dying -- not that I'd die -- death is in the past, but to Lucy Mac and Gerry I'd be dead and I can't quite let go of my deep, deep love for them.

The visualization about the charwomen has shifted. They are now no longer primarily connected with the chemotherapy but they are connected with my immune system. Sometimes I think they are my white blood cells and the construction workers are a part of that internal system that repairs what is broken -- in this case, bones. The charwoman come down the umbilical cord into my body at my navel -- where they are sent to the different cancer sites. At the site they catch cancer cells in a big pouch in their aprons which they zip up. Then they return to my navel and ascend the umbilical cord. I don't know what happens to the cancer "up there." Sometimes the construction workers break through a hardened outer layer of a tumor and scrape out or chip off bits or large blocks of the tumor areas to soften the tumor so it can be scraped out more easily or if there is a cancer cell that clings to the bone wall, the bucket of Navelbine is brought in and the Navelbine is hosed on the cell, which then drops into a charwoman's apron. Then the next charwoman with a scrub brush scours the area free of all traces of the cancer cell.

Sometimes I practice this visualization. More often lately I have found myself simply giving the cancer to God. Actually this is what the visualization is doing -- taking the cancer up the umbilical cord to God.

This morning after breakfast I had an experience that was not new exactly. I had a similar experience at Green Bough, but its recurrence seemed to make it more real. I don't even remember the sequence -- whether I felt open first with all the bones of my body to the substance around me which is God, and to the bird's song, and to the people who surround me, or whether I felt closed first -- closed in the womb -- warm, safe -- closed in the anteroom of the throne room. Suddenly I felt both at the same time -- enclosed in God's womb and open to the air and the birds' songs and the interruptions of the day and God. Not that I can <u>stay</u> that way, but the residue of the experience is still with me. I feel safe in God's deep dark love and open -- like the coral letting the sea enter and exit, flowing through and sustaining its life.

Then an odd picture sequence came to me about the coral. It/I detached from the reef and went free, moving around, except it/I had an umbilical cord-like organ, miles long potentially, that kept it/me attached to the reef. The problem was that all the stubs of coral were floating around and these bits of coral forgot about the umbilical cord and the reef. We ended up all tangled in a huge knot. But I remembered the cord and the reef and I was able to "smallen" myself to the size of the end of the umbilical cord which retracted and landed me safely back in my spot on the coral reef.

Another "rusion" (intrusion) was that at one point I found myself in the anteroom remembering the banquet room next door. I tiptoed in, took a strawberry and ate it. Then the dilemma arose -- what to do with the green cap (of the strawberry). There were no wastebaskets in either room and no cracks in the floor or walls under the seats in the anteroom where I could hide it. I crept back into the banquet room and left it on a side table on a tray. Not long afterwards God's voice asked, "Lucy, did you eat this strawberry?" "Yes," I confessed. Then it was as though God stooped way down and I was a child with no understanding. God asked me gently, "Why did you eat so little?"

Two experiences happened today at church. At one point I had a clear sense that I'd get well, and yet I wouldn't have learned anything, I wouldn't be any different because of this second bout with cancer. I felt very disturbed and without thinking I prayed, "Break my spirit, God." I tried to soften the prayer to, "Mold me and make me after thy will," but the prayer, I knew, had to be harsher -- <u>break</u> was the word. I was reminded of John Donne's "Batter my heart, three-person God". It is a violent poem. "Break my spirit, God"-- like a wild horse that is tamed <u>by God for God's</u> leading, guiding, riding, galloping wildly and freely as I carry God on my back or within me in my broken renewed spirit. "A broken spirit God will not despise" -- especially when God is the breaker.

The second experience focused on the Scripture text for the day, Matt. 22:1-14. I became the wedding guest without a wedding garment. And I felt sheer panic when God said, "Friend, where is your garment?" I knew I had put it on. Had I lost it? Hadn't I done all the right things, prayed for others, entrusted myself to God? How could I not be clothed properly? Then I felt myself searching for what to say. The words from Green Bough's Eucharist (and really from the mass) came to my lips, "I am not worthy, Lord. But say the word and I shall be healed." Beth Thompson after church said, "Isn't life in Christ about being continually reclothed?" Yes -- not what we do but what God does. Not our works but God's grace and our being and doing as they flow from God's grace.

God, grant me the grace to be open and to entrust myself to your womb-love. And, God, break my spirit that we might ride the wind together -- your holy wind.

Oct. 16, 1996 Wed. This morning I lay in the almost hot water of a half-full tub. My left arm lay submerged in the wet heat which bathed the veins seared purple (in my inner elbow) by chemotherapy. The muscles of my back and neck, where cancer-eaten bones are collapsing, relaxed in the warmth. The smell of Orange Cream Bath Oil rose around me; the oil soothed my skin, a gift from seminary spouses I do not really know. Is this suffering, when women my age are long since dead in Nepal from torturous living and women's life expectancy is 41? Is this suffering, when so many wives and mothers in Guatemala and Nicaragua lack potable water for cooking and washing, when these same mothers bring their infants, dead from diarrhea because a simple drug was unavailable? I experience pain -- yes. But I am reluctant to name my battle with cancer "suffering."

November: All Day, All Night Angels Watching Over Me

Nov. 7, 1996. Thur. Daddy keeps insisting that I write this journal

78

whether I feel good or not. But the last 3 weeks I've felt so rotten. I had a 3rd bout with the nausea, vomiting and diarrhea. Marilyn Washburn ended up coming on Sunday afternoon to give me IV fluids, potassium, and some IV nausea medication. Then the next week was okay. I don't talk any more of good days and bad days, only of good hours and bad hours. But on the whole it was an okay week -- chemotherapy on Tuesday or maybe Wednesday. Then Friday Gerry thought I looked funny, felt my head, took my temperature and I had 102.5°. I slept all morning and spent the afternoon at the doctor's office, but no one discovered anything. On Saturday Nancy came for a great low-key two-day visit. Then on Wednesday night I got my 4th bout with the vomiting etc. I went for IV fluids at the doctor's on Thursday. But it was the next Wednesday before I was eating rice and not just fluids. I am still so weak. On Tuesday I told the doctor I couldn't take any more chemotherapy for a while, till I get some strength back.

Some time late last week, Gerry and I were reading our devotional and I remember the psalm urging me to pray simply, "God, save me. Take me. Save me." I prayed that off and on for several days -- especially while I felt so bad. It is interesting that on Sunday Gerry and I decided very clearly it was time to start the ball rolling for my going to the Gerson Institute. Everything fell into place. Peggy can go. Nancy and B and my parents are 100% supportive. I've pondered whether my going is response to my prayer, "Save me." I am a bit nervous that I am doing nothing medically to try to stay the cancer. So many times a day I place myself in God's care. If the cancer takes off wildly, I will accept that as God's will. If the cancer remains quietly in the bones, I will accept that too as God's will. I continue to place myself in God's will, to surrender not just myself but especially the cancer to God.

Nov. 8, 1996. Fri. Dr. Peteet called today to say that the cancer markers in the blood were down. That is the first time since June. He was glad and thinks the Navelbine is working. Maybe it is. But still it is God who is at work and I can continue to entrust myself to God.

I went to school today for my small group in the Baptism Course. I do love the group. The topic was "Spirituality," but it was clear they don't want to discuss spirituality. So I suggested we tell our stories that lie at the base of our spirituality -- those touchstone experiences to which we return again and again, in those moments when we knew God is! And no one can take that certainty from us. I started and told of my experiences of falling into God's love the night before the bone scan. I thought the class was wonderful -- a gorgeous tapestry of stories.

I thought we had hit our first glitch with going to the Gerson Institute today when the travel agent called to say how hard it was working out an upgrade from coach to 1st class. The difference in cost is $475 vs $1600! So we were going to try to use my frequent flyer miles. But the travel agent was having a hard time working it out. This afternoon Catherine and Justo called to offer help and Justo has some transferrable certificates for upgrades. Justo is an "elite" customer with Delta Airlines according to the travel agent. With his help everything worked out finally. I continue to be overwhelmed by the love and support of so many people and by how right this plan to go to the Gerson Institute seems to be.

Nov. 10, 1996 Sun. Oo and B just left a few hours ago -- didn't even stay 24 hours. Golly, was it good to see them. Oo and I had a good visit last night. Becca, Bobby and Debbi were here too. They sat in the kitchen and caucused with Gerry about Ma and G-Daddy. It was a hectic evening but how good it was to visit with B and Oo.

Nov. 11, 1996. Mon. I am trying to write even when there is nothing "significant" to write. Every day I try to start the day with praise to God. I sing the Taize song, "Gloria, Gloria in excelsis deo." Then I recite Psalm 103. I have been reciting through "so that your youth is renewed like the eagles." Lately -- the last two or three days -- I have been going two more verses, "The Lord works vindication for all who are oppressed. He made known his ways to Moses, his acts to the people of Israel." I realized it felt good to be numbered among "the oppressed" -- to belong to a community of the afflicted -- and it was important to hope that my hoped-for deliverance from cancer or from an early death fits a pattern of a God who delivers from slavery, from meaningless living, from fear and sometimes from the pit!

Nov. 12, 1996. Tues. Well, I am reminded that I can't speak of good days and bad days -- only good hours and bad hours. Today was good until just before 6:00 this evening. I had decided to walk down to COH with Gerry for supper. But my back had begun to ache. I took a Darvocet and went down but I must have seemed like a zombie to the group eating. After I finished eating, I left the table and sat in a rocking chair waiting on Gerry. When we got back I was chilled and achy. I turned on the little heater in my alcove and lay sideways on a couple of pillows to ease my back. After a while I found myself talking to God.

I can't reconstruct the conversation, but its content revolved around the three sermons of Walter Brueggemann's I read this morning at the doctor's office, while I was taking aretia to "shore up my bones," as I put it. The first sermon was about Abraham's and Sarah's having Isaac -- a miracle, and the sermon encouraged me to be open to a God of miracles. God can and may work a miracle with my cancer. I guess the sermon shored up the hope for life side of my 50-50 mode of being. The second sermon was about Joseph's revealing himself to his brothers in Egypt and declaring, "God meant it (your selling me into slavery) for good." In my talking to God I realized once again what a Calvinist I am. I prefer to believe God "allowed" my cancer in order to bring much good, and my task is to continue to pray for the grace to be open to that much good. There was a plane crash over India today. Two planes collided and close to 500 persons are presumed dead. Not long ago India suffered severely from a cyclone that hit and killed thousands. I cannot tell the story of any of those who died, who grieve, who struggle to put some measure of life back together after loss. I can only try to interpret my own story and for me it is comforting to think that God has allowed my cancer for a greater good. Maybe such a belief enables me to

81

imagine that <u>maybe</u> I am participating in the suffering of Christ, that what I experience is a fellowship (kinonia) with Christ's suffering.

The third sermon was about God's conversation with Moses out of the burning bush. Walter says God first says, "I, I, I," have seen the suffering of my people; I have heard their cries; I have seen the oppression of the Egyptians. Then God says, "You, you, you" to Moses -- you go, you be my deliverer. I thought about how lately, as my strength returns, I have felt as though I want to be doing some things, not just resting in my alcove or reading. One thing I'd like to do is find a church, probably an Episcopal one, where I can take weekly communion. But that's still for me. I want to find a way to do something for others. I found myself praying that God show me what I might do, because I am not good at thinking up such things on my own. Then I ended by asking God for the grace to entrust myself -- especially my not-so-open heart and my cancer -- to God.

I've been reading <u>Kitchen Table Wisdom</u>. This is in response to "The Emperor's New Clothes" (esp. 95-97). "Dear God, grant me a peaceful death in your own time. Don't let me contribute to its coming too soon, Don't let me fight it when it is time."

<u>Nov. 14, 1996. Thurs</u>. Last night I was thinking again about the boy in <u>Kitchen Table Wisdom</u> who announced, "I'm going home today," threw the medical staff into a tizzy, and then peacefully died that day. I realized I can trust God to call me home in God's own time and God will possibly let me know when that time is. In the meantime I can concentrate on living each day fully, not putting my hopes on any therapy, but on God's gift of each day.

<u>Nov. 16, 1996. Sat</u>. I do nothing so much of the time. Yesterday I went to Columbia Seminary for chapel and communion, talked to a student about a grade, then participated in the Baptism small groups for 2 hours, then talked to a second student about her grade. I came home tired. But today I dozed all morning -- lying down in my sitting area unable to read or to go through my cards and check the list on the computer to see if everyone is on it. I did nothing. And about the

time Gerry came home I was crying, "I'm so useless." I <u>know</u> I am valuable even if all I can "do" is be. But it is so hard to feel valuable when I do so little.

Tonight, doing my sitting, I realized that my image of the "eternal" God is that I am betrothed but my Beloved is gone (an image from Teresa's <u>Interior Castle</u>). But my understanding of the "internal" God is different. God's life is dwelling in me, God is somehow a part of my soul, spirit, internal existence. But I do not have an image of how or what that life looks like. I can image the umbilical cord coming down from God and the charwomen coming and going. I was imaging my "house" closed up to the area in front of the umbilical cord until a few weeks ago -- maybe last week -- when the whole house, like human-made structure collapsed and disappeared. Now there is a clear, fleshly, natural conduit or tube from the umbilical cord to my heart -- but it doesn't seem to me as though the life of God has reached my heart, or at least not very powerfully or influentially. The umbilical cord area also is attached to a deeper part of me, a dark part, I guess near my womb -- but that area is a mystery.

<u>Nov. 19, 1996. Tues</u>. Today I slept till 10:30 (after getting up for breakfast and seeing Lucy Mac off to school). Then I showered and began working on the letters for my non-CTS folks about my going to the Gerson Institute. I sat in the new part of the kitchen to work. During my shower I sang, "All day, all night angels watching over me, my Lord." And at first working on the letters I sang, "On Eagle's Wings." Then I got into the task. It seems when I am sick or energy-less I do a lot of praying. But when I have energy, I don't seem to be as aware of God. I don't like that. I've been trying to pray the "Jesus prayer." Breathe in to "Lord Jesus Christ," breathe out, "have mercy on me." I forgot it. Gerry and I were wondering if we could set an alarm or something to remind us to pray. We'd start up the grandfather clock in the hall but it bongs every 15 minutes and that seems like too often. Probably not really, though.

<u>Nov. 20, 1996. Wed</u>. It seems the more energy I get back the longer

I stay up and the more I do the more my back hurts. Yesterday in addition to the two ibuprofen, I took 2 Darvocets and a Roxicet mid-evening. Today I only took 2 Darvocets plus the 2 ibuprofen but I easily could have taken 3 or I could take one now.

Several times today I remembered to pray the Jesus prayer--. once after I hit my funny bone on my right elbow. It hurt! Still I get real busy doing different tasks and forget about the presence of God. It is hard work but I know it is not work I'm doing alone. If God wants me to be aware of God's presence at all times, then the Holy Spirit has got to be at work more prominently in me to help me be more aware. I pray for the grace to be open to God's Spirit at all times.

<u>Nov. 21, 1996. Fri</u>. I had two interesting insights yesterday. I've been wrestling with the idea or experience of joy. In the <u>Kitchen Table Wisdom</u> book the author writes of the joy she sees in her counselees who have cancer. I couldn't relate at all. Then Sunday we sang, "I've got peace like a river....I've got joy overflowing....I've got the life everlasting." I thought, "I know I have the life everlasting, but I don't understand this joy overflowing." Monday I wept while Gerry listened and sat with me. I know I was getting out my nervousness about going to the Mexican hospital (Gerson Institute), and my frustration with having cancer, but I also kept saying that I didn't have any sense of joy. Somewhere the first of the week I also realized my heart was shut off somehow from God's life flowing within me. I tried to visualize opening my heart to God and I prayed for the grace to be open in my heart to God. Whether that made any difference or not I don't know, but yesterday morning I woke up with a deep sense of joy inside. I believe the "cause" was my realizing if I have life everlasting in my soul, if I belong to God and God's life flows deep within me, then that is cause for joy. At breakfast Lucy Mac yelled at me for trying to help her with the blanket she wraps up in and the spell was broken. But it was there for a few minutes. And all day whenever I was still or aware of my breathing -- which was right often -- I found myself saying the Jesus prayer.

The second insight came late last night when I was doing my sitting. I try to pray every night a form of night prayer with intercessions for those on my prayer list and a time of free prayer when I talk to God. What I have concentrated on in my sitting time has been the part of the opening prayer -- asking for grace to be open and to entrust myself to God. I'd sort of given up on "grace to listen," thinking it meant listening to the crickets and cicadas which I can't hear anymore, or my heart beating which I can't do very well. Suddenly last night I realized my sitting is a time of listening to God, listening for God to speak if and when God so chooses. That insight made my sitting time rich and still, though I wasn't aware of any divine voice.

Nov. 26, 1996. Tues. Peggy and I had a safe trip to Hospital Meridian of Gerson Institute today. Ann Connor on Sunday prayed a wonderful prayer over me, calling this trip a pilgrimage. That has stuck with me as an accurate grace-filled image. I have been and am surrounded by the Holy. I am here to discern God's moving in my life, my body, my spirit. Praise be to God.

Nov. 28, 1996. Thurs. Thanksgiving. I've had a high pulse rate -- still I think I've had it since June. So they can't give me coffee enemas which really are supposed to detox me. The chamomile tea enemas are doing some good, Peggy says. There are a few dregs of coffee in them. Then today I was told I'm anemic and have a fever of 101°, then 102.2°, then 99°.

Last night I woke up and realized I have to grieve the loss of a life-style. This will be a long process -- maybe over 2 years of the full Gerson regimen -- partly because of the chemotherapy and partly because of how long it takes bones to heal. And this regimen is so different, so strange. I cried this afternoon, saying, "I don't want to be here," I daydreamed about going to the airport and trying to go home. And as often as I remembered I prayed as I breathed in and out, "Lord Jesus Christ -- have mercy on me." I also prayed that God grant me the grace to entrust myself -- my body, spirit, the cancer --

to God.

I had a dream night before last that I held a baby boy in my lap. I hit it hard, very hard, then I lifted it up and tried to comfort its crying. I'm crying now as I write this. I'm the baby who is hit and whom I'm trying to comfort. I've thought a few times of Psalm 131 -- I have calmed and quieted my spirit like a weaned child on its mother's breast. May God be my mother so that I can lean for comforting on God's breast.

This morning I had the insight that not just this trip but all of life is a pilgrimage -- a searching for the holy -- everywhere, in the extraordinary and the ordinary.

Nov. 29, 1996. Friday. (Peggy as scribe) I've felt real weepy all day, real weird and sad. This morning after breakfast I found myself asking God if I could just have a little bit of time with God today. Several times I tried to do my "sitting" -- lying down -- and I fell asleep. I also found myself praying the Jesus prayer over and over and over again. This morning I think what triggered it was that my glass of orange juice was only about ⅔ full, and the companions' were full, and the glasses for some rooms were only about ½ full. It occurred to me they might be gradually cutting back on orange juice they give us, and it's the only thing they give us that I really like and look forward to. This afternoon what triggered it was that I'd had a good conversation with Lucy Mac and Gerry on the phone. Lucy Mac was in good spirits, but Gerry has been worried about me all day. I had just had an ozone enema when he called, so toward the end of the conversation I felt a need to go to the bathroom. I decided to wait until the conversation was over. No sooner had we hung up, than the nurse came in to put in a temporary IV and to give me Laetrile. I felt so sad and beat-up. And then the lights went out, and that threw the schedule all off. I refused to eat any supper or drink my juice, and the doctor gave me apple sauce and will send me apple juice.

Some time after the nurses left this afternoon, I had a kind of daydream that I was in hydrotherapy (where they turn the water up very high and try to increase your internal temperature. The doctor talked about scheduling it for me tomorrow.) With my temperature so high in the afternoon, it went up too high, and I scrambled out of the tub. I think I was shouting, and I fell into Peggy's arms and died. And God said, "You've got to go back. You've got 20 years or more to live. Do the best you can." A little while after I had the same daydream.

Tonight following a conversation with Peggy (who said she thought my body was on the side of the cancer), I imaged the cancer and the therapy engaging in a tennis match, and I was sitting right at the net as a kind of net judge, watching the match but not taking sides. Suddenly I got up and joined the therapy on its side and was given a tennis racquet; but I don't like tennis, so it shifted to ping-pong, and then to badminton, which Peggy and I used to play as doubles partners in college. Somewhere along the line, the match got too active, and I had to sit out, but I was still on the side of therapy. (End of Peggy as scribe.)

Nov. 30, 1996 Sat. Last night I had three dreams/visions that came while I lay awake or in the dropping-into-and-out-of-sleep state. In the first I saw a huge statue of Jesus like the one in Rio de Janeiro, except the arms weren't stretched out, they were near his chest. I was drawn into his arms and held tight to his chest. Then I looked over the city. It was night and the lights sparkled. "Jesus," I said, "Do you hear the cries of all those who suffer from here?" "Yes," he said. "And what do you do?" "I send the Holy Spirit." "And what then?" I asked. "Some accept the Spirit and some do not." "Why is that?" I asked. "That is a question you will have to ask God when you see God face to face." "And me, do I have the Holy Spirit?" "Of course," he said tenderly. "In my heart?" I persisted. "Ah," said Jesus very tenderly, "You are a hard one -- so many heart-thoughts and head-thoughts of your own."

In the second "vision" I was walking along the corridor here at the hospital and ran hard into the glass wall of the nurses' station. The glass barely fractured but the blow shattered my neck and back bones. I fell to the floor dead. Pondering this as I lay awake, I realized that my current ego pattern has to die in order to be reshaped into something new. Like Soleil in my fairy tale.

The third waking dream was more a rationalization -- that the womb of God is my heart where God is trying to birth a new "me." I at some point wondered if I am to help Jesus with the suffering of the city and its resistance to the Holy Spirit.

This morning Peggy and I read (no, Peggy read to me) Bible passages of healing in Matthew and my 3 passages -- Psalms, John and Romans. Then we prayed together. It was very precious time.

It is almost lunch time. I became aware about an hour ago that I have been moderately depressed since I went on the chemotherapy in the summer. I can get out of my depression to lead my small group at school or to go to church or community. But I have had no energy for reading or cross-stitching. I'd spend most of my time resting. This nutrition approach to wellness has been Gerry's idea so I've let him bring me my carrot juices -- or not -- at home. I've played the victim. I'm doing the same here. Peggy has tried to learn to do the enemas; she went to the B-12 liver shot demo this morning. I've realized I need to be more pro-active -- by the grace of God. I've got to learn to give myself the shots and the enemas and to make the juices. I'm not there yet but maybe by God's grace -- by the Holy Spirit Jesus sends to those of us who cry out -- maybe I'll get there.

December: Ain't Gonna Let Nobody Turn Me Around

Dec 2, 1996. Mon. (Peggy as scribe) Yesterday was a good day, but today I've had vomiting, diarrhea and nausea. Sometimes I think this is not about fighting cancer or healing from cancer or dying from cancer. It is about birthing in me a deeper and more faithful soul.

I had another vision or daydream today -- a waking dream: I was concerned about all the food in the kitchen going to the compost pile at the end of the day. So I planned for it to be distributed to the poor. The site was down at the abandoned school Peggy and I have walked by, and I saw myself and many others carrying pots of leftover goods down to the school. At some point I either tripped or was tripped and a beggar boy stole my pot. Immediately I was on my feet again, but I fell once more and everyone in the line started walking over me -- hundreds of people walking over me. Then I found myself beside a wall, sitting on the sidewalk, the line of people and pots still going by. Then I was encircled and lifted up by the countless prayers of those praying for me. The prayers carried me to the statue of Jesus, who held me. Jesus reminded me that he was the healer and that he could use any means he wanted. I was feeling nauseated at the time, and Jesus put his hand through my body and into my stomach. The nausea didn't go away, but I felt calm. Then Jesus said, "I could cure you with a touch," and began stroking the inside of every bone where there was cancer. I lay there as Jesus stroked the cancerous bones.

Some time later I had this very brief experience of awareness that God is everywhere and that I was somehow right there with God. I am not explaining it very well at all.

It's odd to me that when I feel so bad I'm much more aware of God than on a good day like yesterday. No, when I feel bad, I'm much more listening to God. It is as though I am being moved to a place where all my life is sitting time -- time when I am yearning for the grace of gratitude, praise and joy, and the grace to listen, to be open, and to entrust myself to God. At one point I found myself in a thorough state of listening -- listening to my body, listening to odd sounds in the environment, and listening to God. (End of Peggy as scribe)

Dec. 4, 1996. Wed. I'm better tonight. I seem to be moving through a cycle of this illness faster here -- but the last 2½ days have been no fun. Peggy and I have been continuing our daily devotions -- reading from the Bible a number of selections like a series of healing stories from the Gospel, one of many psalms and sometimes a chapter from John and Romans plus prayers. The ritual has been very important.

Several days ago, maybe as far back as Saturday, I realized that if I were to cooperate with this therapy, God would have to turn me around. Those 3 words conjured up a COH (civil rights) song. I began singing off and on -- "Ain't gonna let nobody turn me around, turn me around, turn me around. Ain't gonna let nobody turn me around; gonna keep on walking, keep on talking, marching into freedom land." I would sing the first of this song and add "except God." And yet I knew part of me was resisting being turned around in a major way. Today I began to reconstruct the song in a way that, I hope, reflects my gradual acceptance of this regimen: "Dear God of Jesus, turn me toward life; Dear God of Jesus, turn me toward life so I can keep on loving, keep on praising, working for shalom." I started off trying, "Oh, God in heaven." But that made God too far off. The image of God as the God of Jesus came, I am sure, from Peggy's reading to me healing story after healing story in the Gospels.

Dec. 6, 1996. Fri. Last night I had an experience it will be hard to describe. Peggy and I had an eventful afternoon and evening giving me two enemas. We had both slept soundly during the day because the night before I had been up vomiting one last time, so we were both awake late into the night resting in the dark. For devotions Peggy had read Psalm 51, and from the psalm in the still darkness, there arose within me the phrase -- "a broken spirit." I knew my spirit was broken. I remember the prayer I had prayed earlier (Oct. 13), "Break my spirit, God." Here I was -- a broken spirit -- completely open, without any sense of desire or need to do anything. I rested in that profound broken-openness. Then the nurse came in to give me a pill for diarrhea. He said he'd come back at 12 midnight with a shot for nausea. I was snippy with him -- said I didn't want a shot and hadn't had nausea. Afterwards, as I lay again in the dark quiet, I realized the broken spirit that had been briefly open to God and life in the new way had vanished. I was sorry for being ugly to the nurse and I even realized this morning that a shot from him meant an injection into my IV line, not into my muscle (my catheter had been removed earlier this evening so I took the nausea medicine by mouth). This morning I had the same experience of broken-openness again. I was lying on my bed resting -- both Peggy and I are very tired (I had another diarrhea pill at 5:00 AM). Suddenly I felt empty, transparent, completely open.

90

It is a way of being that I pray I can cultivate as I move from meditation into active living and interacting with people. It is a way of being that seems correct to a hospitable heart. Both last night and this morning my ears had been pounding, but for the duration of the experience they were absolutely silent. It was as though I had emerged into some still center.

Dec. 20, 1996. Fri. If there is one thing I came back from Mexico (the Gerson Institute) with, it is hope. Hard-won hope, that came to me as a divine gift in the valleys of gargantuan shadows where tears and prayers fell freely. But in the end God's gift to me was hope. Hope. I've said again and again since I've been back, "I'd rather live with hope than without it." One day God may whisper in my ear, "This is sickness unto death." Or one day there may be an accident and I awake with God. If there is time to prepare myself and those I love for my death, I will do so then. But until then, I believe God wants me to live each day, each hour fully -- both for God and with God.

Dec. 21, 1996. Sat. I've discovered that for me one of the most faithless things I can say is, "This too shall pass" (a saying in a '60s song that was supposed to summarize wisdom). In each moment I am living the life God has given me. To wish it away is to wish away God's gift with all its hidden treasures.

This morning, I had no energy and stayed in bed. When I did get up, around 2:00 PM, I was very weepy. I'm better now. I am going to try to grade some papers.

January-February: Gloria

Jan. 1, 1997. Wed. Peggy stayed a week and helped us get lots of the regimen set up. She did a lot of shopping with Louie. Then B came and spent a week including Christmas. He and Gerry did a lot of plumbing and running a heat vent to the new bathroom. Then he left. Now it's just the family. We are trying. Dean does most of the cooking for me; Louie does the shopping; Gerry does the setting out of meals and pills and the juices -- we manage 2 or 3 carrot juices a day; and I do the enemas. I'm getting in one 20-ounce enema a day usually. It's hard. I've had next to no energy and had lost 3 more pounds last Friday in the 2 weeks I've been home from Mexico. We called Dr. Garcia who let me add to my diet rice twice a week, lentils 3 times a week and white-fish filet Monday, and it was absolutely delicious with lemon on it.

When I'm so weak, I find myself singing "Gloria" several times a day, but doing my sitting is hard and writing in this journal is hard. I have so little energy that I barely manage to read my mail. I haven't answered any letters in a long time. The last few days I have seemed to have a bit more energy -- since the fish filet! Yesterday and today I worked with Gerry on the index for my book. I only rested twice and took two Roxicets late in the afternoon. (I've been taking 4 or 2 plus 2 Darvocets.)

Tonight I was reading Lucy Mac a story of a man who depended on God for everything. The story was encouraging people to pray for what they need. I found myself later praying for healing and rallying my life-forces around the prayer, trying to meet God's healing energy with my own faith and commitment.

Jan. 3, 1997. Fri. I stay so weak and spend so much time in bed. Some days I get discouraged and cry a bit out of frustration. Peggy reminded me tonight on the phone that I have said my being sick has brought me closer to God. Lately I haven't been so aware of God. But I want to pray more that God will help me with the grace of listening to God, being open to God, and entrusting myself to God as well as the grace of gratitude, praise and joy. At times I feel all of the graces and relax peacefully. But at other times I get very discouraged by the regimen. Peggy also reminded me that my larger hope for getting well is to see Lucy Mac grow up, to move into old age with Gerry, to do my part for God's coming shalom, and to glorify God each day. Those are still my deepest prayers.

92

Jan. 10, 1997. Fri. Berta came for a visit yesterday. Depending on the weather (snow and ice are forecast) she will stay till Monday. We've had a good day today. I've had a good amount of energy, though it has taken me 4 Roxicets and I'll probably take 2 more before I go to bed. I had fish and it was so satisfying (I hope I cooked it long enough). I've tried to be aware of God today and I've done pretty well. I don't want to put myself under pressure to be in an awareness of God all my waking hours -- I keep praying for the grace to listen to God, be open to God, and entrust myself to God.

Jan. 25, 1997. Sun. I haven't written in weeks because I've felt as though I've been on a plateau. Sometimes feeling good and a bit energetic; sometimes sleeping whole days at a time. I try to remember to ask God for discernment and help with the regimen. Sometimes at lunch or supper I look at the potato on my plate and cry. Sometimes -- especially when I've been sleeping most of the day -- I can't hold the enema. I get frustrated so often at these times. I try to cling to God or relax into the prayers and thoughts of those who care about me. Sometimes it is so hard.

Last week B came to spell Gerry, who went to Florida to be with his father and visit his Mom. It was a hard visit for him. His dad is declining, it seems.

I keep trying every morning to sing Gloria and recite either Psalm 121 or the first verses of Psalm 103. Gerry and I don't do our prayers since he got back last Thursday, nor am I doing my sitting regularly. Next Sunday I plan to become an associate member at Green Bough, but I don't feel very spiritual.

Jan. 28, 1997. Wed. Today felt like a crucial day. Last Sunday after supper and before Community of Hospitality worship I threw up my supper. I had been hovering between 106 lbs. and 109 lbs. in my weight, but after Sunday night I felt as though I was losing ground and couldn't recover it. We've tried calling Dr. Garcia since Monday night, but she hasn't returned our calls or is very busy when we call. I haven't been drinking the carrot or green juices except one carrot juice in the morning. My weight fell to 104 and I felt as though if I lost any more weight and got any weaker I'd die. Gerry has been reading about cancer therapies and he read that ⅔rds of cancer patients die from wasting away -- getting so weak something other than the cancer kills them. He has been very anxious the last few days that the cancer is robbing me of all the nutrition I'm eating so that my cells aren't getting any nutrients. Since we couldn't get Dr. Garcia, he talked to a friend who recommended and sold him some medicine called hydrazine-sulfate. I started taking it Tuesday morning. It is supposed to help with weight gain in 50% of those who use it. This morning I had the clear sense that I was dying -- wasting away and too weak to eat. Gerry and I cried together a lot. I prayed off and on while we cried together. Basically I wanted help entrusting our lives to God -- Lucy Mac's, Gerry's, mine, Dean's, Louie's. I found myself far more worried about Lucy Mac and Gerry than about myself. At one point I asked Gerry if I died, would he raise Lucy Mac? He said, of course, why? And I told him I was afraid he would die too, if I did. He replied that that was why he was trying to take care of himself physically. This afternoon I read an Agatha Christie mystery -- totally got myself away from myself, and took 2 Roxicets about 6:00 PM. By 6:50 or so when I finished the mystery, I was feeling much better. I ate a lot of supper, which I took to the healing prayer group's meeting in the computer room. I didn't cry talking about the day -- a sign I felt stronger -- until the prayers we prayed for folks touching Gerry and me. I know just because I feel strong tonight is no indication of how I'll feel tomorrow. But I pray that my appetite and weight will improve steadily.

Feb. 10, 1997. Mon. I still have good hours and bad hours. Last week B came back and helped me through the beginning of school. Gerry went to Green Bough for a retreat -- it was a good break for him.

I've several things to record. I've been saying Psalm 121 many mornings, after I sing Gloria. And I've been pondering the lines, "The Lord shall preserve thee from all evil; he shall preserve thy soul." Well, if cancer is evil, then that first line is a lie. God didn't preserve me from evil. Psalm 91 has similar claims and the evil came right into my tent. But maybe cancer is not evil -- since sickness and death are a part of life -- at least physical death. Maybe the parallel line about God's preserving my soul provides a key to understanding the line about evil. Maybe the evil is that which threatens to destroy the soul -- and cancer can certainly be a vehicle for evil's attacking and terrifying the soul. But my cancer doesn't terrify me. It makes me cry and it makes me aware of how much I would miss of my life if I died soon, but it is nowhere near harming my soul, and for that I praise God.

I reread the screen play of <u>Cabaret</u> and summarized it for a contribution I may make to the volumes Jana and I are finishing up editing. The Scripture passages are Matthew and Romans, reminding Christians to wake up. I got to musing if cancer is a wake up call to me. Wow? And I realized I've been praying more spontaneously and frequently lately --- asking God for help in eating and thanking God for each bite that stays down. (I've been nauseated lately by some foods.) And I am trying to be very grateful for each day and for my waking times. I sleep a lot. I began to say to myself, "I'm dying -- maybe not in the next few months-- but maybe so, maybe not in the next few years -- but maybe so, maybe not in the next ten years, but maybe so. I am dying -- how can I live the gift of this day?

<u>Feb. 11, 1997. Tues.</u> Last night I did my sitting lying down from 10:40 to 11:00. At first I relaxed into the realization that for me at some level it doesn't matter how long I live, but how I live each day. That was a comforting realization.

Then later I found myself concentrating on trying to listen to God.

Within the last month or two an image of my heart has shifted. At first God's love and presence were crashing against the stone walls of my heart like ocean waves on a castle. Then one time the water went over the walls and I realized my heart was an aquarium tank that needed the water. The incoming water began to revive all the languishing plants and animals in my heart. Then the image shifted so

95

that the aquarium walls first became perforated and then disappeared so that my heart linked by means of the ocean water to every other heart. Last night there was no change in this image, just a soothing sense that my heart is an eddy of the ocean that is God's loving presence for all people.

Toward the end of my sitting as I focused on the words, "Listen to God," I had the experience of God as a voice beginning to say something to me. I projected that it was something about how long I have to live, so I interrupted and said, "I don't want to know." The voice replied, "Listen to me." So I tried to make myself as open as possible to what God might have to say. Suddenly God became a huge jet black presence that lifted me up into the divine arms and held me tightly. "I love you," God said. "I know," I answered, beginning to fill with tears. "I delight in your being," God said. "In my being?" I asked. "In your being, and in your doing. I delight in your being and your being's issuing in doing." I lay still, feeling unbelievable joy and then the experience faded.

Today a home-nurse came to take some blood so that tomorrow they can give me a blood transfusion.

<u>Feb. 16, 1997. Sun</u>. Mary Bailey Davis died last night of pancreatic cancer. Murphy called this morning. She said her mother could hear what was said to her right to the end. They knew she died sometime during the night. Her husband was with her. The end was easy -- a slipping away.

I pray for a peaceful death and her death reminds me God does take care of God's own. I pray my death is neither too soon nor too late -- but according to God's time. I sometimes want to die and be with God fully. I understand Paul. But I believe I am needed here with Lucy Mac, Gerry, Dean and Louie. I want to live and be with them and praise my God here as long as I am given breath and life.

March: My Jesus I Love Thee

<u>March 7, 1997. Fri</u>. It is hard for me to write when things seem on a

96

plateau or when my two speeds are 35 mph for school and being with Lucy Mac, and 0 mph when I lie in bed. Also when B or Nancy is visiting, I'd rather spend "good" time with them -- or with Gerry in the evenings.

In the down times of tears and a deep sense of wasting away, I have found that I cling to the prayers of those praying for me and let them hold me close to God's heart. I also pray for the grace to entrust myself to God. Gerry is so good to me in these times -- taking me seriously, not being accusatory.

A few weeks ago I had another profound sense of God's saying almost audibly, "If you get well it is my healing." That experience freed me to remember that the diet and the daily enemas are for me, not for them. I'm trying to discern God's will and listen to my body more, not trying to follow a regimen strictly as though the power to heal were in the regimen.

About 10 days ago I was meditating and the phrase I was using to help me stay focused was the prayer for grace to be open. Suddenly it occurred to me I wasn't open to God's healing touch. (We had been studying Matt. 9:18-21 in class.) I prayed that God grant me the grace to be open to God's healing touch. Immediately a light entered my head -- illuminating the base of my skull, my neck and radiating through my shoulders to my right arm, continuing down my back and around into the ribs as it proceeded downward -- into my pelvic bones and ending in my upper legs. The experience was more a visualization than a physical sensation, but it was very real. The next night the same areas in the same procedure were touched by a rich, almost liquid blackness. Subsequent nights I experienced a rainbow of colors and yellow. A few nights ago as I was meditating, I "felt" God's own finger following the course of the cancer areas down my back.

Last night the "substance" was red -- blood, as though it were the blood of Jesus.

I've also had a sense of deep peacefulness in my better hours. Last night I found myself crying because a rash on my sides and back hurt from itching and my scratching, and I cried that I didn't want to

97

die. But often I find myself grateful to be alive, and grateful for Lucy Mac and Gerry and Dean and Louie, and work and colleagues and people who care about me. Tonight brushing my teeth I found myself singing, "My Jesus, I love Thee." Now and again I find. myself saying, "God, I love you."

Every morning for a long time now I continue to try to sing Gloria, Gloria, before I get up, as well as to say Psalm 121 or the first verses of Psalm 103.

<u>Mar. 17, 1997. Mon</u>. There is lots to write. I don't know why so often there is no motivation. I think it was later in the evening the last time I wrote that I had this experience during my sitting. I was curled up like a scarab on the floor in the anteroom on a pattern on the floor that seemed just made for me -- an oval area designated by the mosaic of the floor which just fit my crouched body. The door to the throne room opened and God said, "Come in." I knew that meant I was to get up and walk in and I didn't want to. I started crying violently, "No, no. I can't." I kept crying. The throne room was silent; the door remained ajar. Finally I crept in and immediately crouched down in my scarab position. "Stand up," God said very gently. Again I began to cry violently. "I can't," I sobbed. Silence. After a while, I stood up. "I love you," God said. "I know," I replied. "I delight in you." "I know that." "I will heal you." "No," I cried, "Don't say that. Don't say that." I cried and cried. I couldn't go on with the imaging. I asked Gerry if he was asleep and told him what had happened, continuing to cry and saying as I told him God's last words, "I don't believe it." I'm sure at some level I'm wrestling with Jesus' words to the woman with the flow of blood, "Your faith has saved you/or made you whole/well."

When I finally went back to bed, I had 10 more minutes of sitting to do, so I tried to return to my sitting mode although I'm lying down. Two things happened that I remember now. One was God's saying, "If you are a temple of the Holy Spirit, then you are a temple of me." The other experience was of swimming or being drawn down deep inside myself, not in a blood vessel, but in a channel or tube of some kind. Down, down. I was aware of not being afraid of drowning. Finally I got to the crossroads where about 5 channels came together. In the intersection I curled up in a fetal position and lay still.

A few nights ago Gerry and I watched the first tape of Bill Moyers' series on Healing and the Mind. The tape focuses on Chinese medicine and particularly the Chinese understanding of "chi" (translated roughly "life-force"). Chi's center is just below the belly button and it flows through the body along its own channels. Sickness is the result of blocked chi. One can find one's chi by meditating, and medicine is about getting chi flowing healthfully again. The source or center of chi was just about the same spot where I'd "arrived," which I'd called an intersection. The night we saw the video in my sitting I went back to that spot -- it was empty -- no chi. The next night I went back again. This time chi flowed in like a tidal wave, carrying me in front of it at a tremendous speed. Then it was as though the chi said, "'Why are you so small? Why isn't your sense of you spread throughout your body?" Then the chi began to grind me up -- with my consent -- like the ocean grinds up sand and shells along its shores in the breakers. And the chi distributed "me" throughout my body and even slightly beyond my body. Then I realized chi isn't "mine"; it doesn't reside in me. It is a life force that flows through me like the ocean/God that flows through the swaying coral. Suddenly the chi inside me became countless moons reflecting God's light. God said, "I am the darkness, I am light; in the light I am darkness. Don't be afraid to explore me under the guise of light." And these chi-moons gathered in the places where the cancer tumors are and covered them up completely. Last night the chi-moons were still there.

This afternoon God said,"Get up." I was resting and had been most of the day. I started crying, "No, I can't." It is as though I am being encouraged to be more active -- not that being isn't sometimes all that is required of me -- but could I be more active? Marilyn Washburn encouraged me to exercise. I could work out minimally on the Nordic track without stressing my back. Such moving might be easier on my back than real walking. And I do want at some level to get back to reading John and Paul for how they speak to my emerging understanding of God and suffering and life. And is God asking me to be more active in my own healing? Whatever that means. I deeply dislike the books that have cures for cancer if I simply follow their suggestion. I'd be taking hundreds of pills a day. I have enjoyed Larry Dossey's Healing Words about the therapeutic value of prayer and the implication that the best prayer is "Thy will be done" plus getting on with life. I've been praying in effect, "Thy will be done," when I pray for the grace to entrust myself to God. Maybe these recent conversations with God are about its being time I do a little more about getting on with life. I'll pray for discernment.

Also this afternoon I revisited a switch inside me that points toward life, or up. Maybe it is reminiscent of the tennis match between healing or life and the cancer. To the left is life and I guess on the switch or in the court to the right is cancer or giving up. The two directions I saw this afternoon were up -- I guess a kind of neutral position -- and left toward life. The switch was pointing up. I tried to push the switch left, but couldn't. A voice said, "I'll do that," and a huge hand easily switched the pointer to life.

Mar. 18, 1997. Tues. Late last night as I "sat" and asked for grace to listen openly and trustingly to God, the image of the chi-moons returned. This time they weren't all silver as they had been the first time. They were gold and iridescent like precious gems. They sparkled as they covered the cancerous parts of my bones.

Then the image switched. I was a creator of bonsai. I had a 3 inch evergreen tree whose branches I had wired to make it look as though it had weathered many, many storms. The tree sat on the top of a large rock between 2 and 3 feet high and 14 to 18 inches wide. As I began the process of working with this tree, the dirt almost covered the top of the rock so that the tree's roots dangled down around the rock, finding dirt and water for living on top of the rock. Slowly as the roots grew longer, I brushed away the dirt, a little at a time, slowly over the years until the tree on top -- still the same size -- had roots hanging all the way down the rock's sides until they reached the dirt and water at the very bottom of the rock. Once I took the bonsai to

100

a show. Someone asked me, "How long have you been working with this tree?" "Thirty-five years," I answered. "Since I was fifty." The tree sat in a fairly shallow pottery piece especially made for it. One time the pot got too small. I had an exact replica made only bigger. With help I set the tree-rock and first pot into the second pot. Then I broke the first pot so the roots had room to stretch and grow around the shards of the first pot.

As I reflected on this experience, I suddenly realized I am the bonsai tree, my roots are being forced to grow longer and longer in my search for nourishment and life. And a strange realization also occurred to me that the rock is God. God may also be the bonsai artist, creator, the soil, the air -- but the major part God is playing in this scenario is rock. I don't know much at all of what that means.

Mar. 25, 1997. Wed. Just a few insights and experiences. Last Wednesday at healing prayer I read my entry for March 17th. The group used my words for comments on how they see me doing and for reflections on their own lives. Sally Brown and Peter were there, having eaten supper with us. Sally said she saw my experiences with the chi and with God as an invitation to reclaim the holy space that is my body. I want to ponder that further. Last night during my sitting I had the image of myself as a lighthouse, only the light was in my heart and that light was reflected outward by huge reflectors in my head and arms and feet. At the same time, it was also as though I glowed with light in a way that assured me all my body is important and to be valued -- not just my heart or my mind.

Last Sunday I think while I was doing an enema and bouncing my lower torso to try to help keep the enema in, I found myself bouncing fast to the tune of Cabaret, which we had watched Saturday night. Suddenly I quit singing Cabaret in my head and began singing Gloria, Gloria. My bouncing slowed and my whole internal pace became a crawl. A peacefulness settled over me. Somehow shifting from Cabaret to Gloria exemplifies something of what it means to one to wake up and become aware of the holy dimension of life no matter what I'm doing, to surrender myself at all times to praising God.

Last night during my sitting, as I just wrote, I enjoyed mulling over, surrendering to the image of the lighthouse. At some point I remembered the Russian pilgrim cautioning that meditating by means of images is a lower form of meditation. And I remember thinking, "Oh well, if I haven't gotten very far down this road called spirituality, that's okay. I love the images that ease into my consciousness from somewhere beyond and that I imagine to be gifts from God."

April: I Am Thine, O Lord

<u>April 5, 1997. Sat</u>. Yesterday during one of the sermons[1] a student read the story (I think from Isaiah, although I think it is also in II Kings) about Hezekiah's illness. Isaiah went to Hezekiah who was lying on his bed and told him he was going to die. I immediately felt a deep identification with Hezekiah. Isaiah left and Hezekiah turned his face to the wall and prayed. He reminded God of how faithful he'd been and what good works he had done. It was prayer that I as a Calvinist (deeply aware of my sinful nature that taints even the best actions and intentions) would never pray. Nevertheless I let Hezekiah's words be my words. God heard Hezekiah's prayer, spoke to Isaiah and sent the prophet back to the king. Isaiah told Hezekiah he had 15 more years to live, and that he would recover in 3 days. Then he gave instructions for a healing poultice and went away. I heard the promise of 15 years as though the words had been spoken to me and I quietly asked God what is the poultice for my cancer? Today I opened a note from Cousin Claiborne. It contained information about a number of alternative medicine experiments being conducted at UCLA. One is for people whose breast cancer has metastasized to the bone. Tears welled up spontaneously -- my poultice, I wondered. I'll call the number on Monday. Then Allison, Jonathan's mother, gave me the number of a nurse who is interested

---

[1] This entire Spring Lucy regularly taught classes in Preaching at Columbia Seminary.

in and knowledgeable about nutrition and cancer. Another part of the poultice? It was a Friday when I heard and believed the word. In the Hebrew calculation of time the third day would be Sunday: crucifixion on Friday, resurrection on Sunday, the third day. Then one other parallel event occurred to me -- and I laughed. Hezekiah asked Isaiah for a sign -- How would he know he would recover? Isaiah asked if the king wanted the sun to go forward or backward. The king answered, "Backward." Well, tonight is the night we shift the clocks forward an hour -- the sun going forward, granted artificially but what a strange coincidence or sign from God.

By God's grace I will not be angry with God if I do not live 15 more years, but I do feel more surely on the side of life, of living deeply, joyfully, faithfully each day to the best of my ability.

Kathleen O'Connor came by for a visit this afternoon. She told me of a book written by a man living with cancer who has collected stories of illness and organized them into 3 categories. One, those in which the doctor or a medicine will cure the disease (I think I was there last summer). Two, stories that reflect chaos. No narrative emerges but instead small unconnected snippets of action. And third, narratives in which the persons expect to find meaning in and through the illness. Sometimes I'm in the chaos and Gerry is so wonderful to let me cry my way through to the other side. He just holds me and I can talk or not as the waves of chaos and fear swell and quieten. And a lot of the time I believe I am in the midst of the third type of narrative -- a narrative of life that has unrepeatable meaning in God's promised shalom.

Apr. 6, 1997. Sun. An important part of the Hezekiah story I forgot is Isaiah's prophecy to Hezekiah that on the third day he would go to the house of the Lord. Today is the third day and I, too, went to the House of the Lord today. It was good to be back at Clifton after having missed the last two or three weeks.

Apr. 11, 1997. Fri. I was taking a shower a few minutes ago and I started crying as I often do. I told myself I was grieving and the question arose, "Grieving for what? The stress you had before this?" And I turned to God and asked, "Why am I crying?" An answer came -- "It is as though you think you're drowning but the water is your home."

I remembered a hymn I used to sing to God, "I am thine, O Lord, I have heard thy call, and thy power and grace divine. But I long to rise in the arms of faith and my will be lost in thine." (That's not quite right, I don't think) But it goes on, "Draw me nearer, nearer, nearer, blessed Lord, to thy precious bleeding side. Draw me nearer, nearer, nearer, blessed Lord, to thy precious bleeding side." My first sermon in Aberdeen, NC, was "Be careful what you ask for, because one day you will get it, and you'll have to live with it." I don't want to be anywhere else except close to Jesus' bleeding side, share his suffering for the sake of God's promised shalom. But I wonder if I hadn't prayed that hymn, would my life be different now? More superficial as I believe it was before? Or was that the Holy Spirit praying within me -- directing me to the life God so deeply wants me to live in God and with God's beloved children? I remember I used to wonder how God would answer the prayer.

Apr. 26, 1997. Sat. Yesterday I listened to the first set of second sermons by my students. One of the passages was Paul's description of the armor we're to wear (in Ephesians). If I remember correctly, the passage urges us to stand. Last night during my meditating time, I found myself standing before God in the throne room. I tried curling up like a scarab on the floor but standing felt better -- seemed more faithful. But I found myself bowing my head. Something drew me forward so that I rested my head on God's knees. Then God invited me to sit beside God on the throne -- on God's left. The throne stretched to make room for me. I looked out into the room and saw that the door into the anteroom was ajar and a long thin ray of light streamed in. Then the door closed and it was pitch black. "What do you do in the darkness?" I asked God. "I have the whole universe inside me," came the answer. "I pay attention to what's going on." "But I'm outside, sitting here," I said puzzled. "You're inside me and

104

outside me, just as I am inside you and outside you." When I began to get sleepy, I laid my head on God's lap and fell into a deeply restful sleep. (Although in reality I was awake much of the night with pain in my chin. But even lying awake was restful for me.)

A Prayer

(This is a prayer which Lucy had stuck in her Journal. She apparently liked it very much.)

Prayer of Abandonment
by Brother Charles of Jesus

Father, I abandon myself into Your hands;
Do with me what You will.

Whatever You may do, I thank You.
I am ready for all, I accept all.

Let only Your will be done in me,
And in all Your creatures --
I wish no more than this, O Lord.

Into Your hands I commend my soul.
I offer it to You with all the love of my heart,
For I love You, Lord,
And need to give myself,
to surrender myself into Your hands
without reserve,
and with boundless confidences;
For You are my Father.

Chapter 3

Letters by Lucy to Friends & Family

Letter #1   July 18, 1996

Dearest friends on the Seminary Campus:

Thanks for the vegetables!

Also thanks for the all-year lollipop and PT Bear. Lucy Mac started eating the sucker, but hasn't put a dent in it. PT lives in the alcove next to my bed/sitting area when Lucy Mac isn't playing with him. He is a constant reminder of your thoughts, prayers, support, and affection.

The new hormone medicine the doctor has me on seems to be lessening the pain, so that I have cut back substantially on the pain medication. Consequently I am functioning more lucidly and actually feeling good.

I also find myself, for the most part, living each day with a profound sense of peacefulness and joy. In the past few days I have come to an odd realization. If I had the choice of erasing the last month and a half and continuing on as before or being where I am now, having lived through the catastrophe of the last six weeks, I would choose being where I am now. I have felt the love of God so tangibly, as though I were immersed or engulfed or bound up in God's faithful love. Several times a day I am moved to surrender myself to that love. Then I can entrust my heart and my body to that love, I can entrust those I love to that love, I can rest in that love, and I become aware of a deep sense of connectedness with all people and God's creation. As I return to many of my former activities, I pray this peacefulness remains.

May the peace of Christ be with each of you that you may glorify and enjoy God each day.

Love,

Lucy

Dear Nancy,[1]   Aug. 16, 1997

Thanks for your letter. I've not been much in the mood to answer my notes and letters lately (I think I've gotten 90 or 100). But it's Friday night; Gerry went to Home Depot to buy something for our renovated bathroom, Lucy Mac's watching *America's Funniest Home Videos*; and, I don't know, answering your letter seemed like the thing I wanted to do.

You said you'd be interested in passages of scripture that have been sustaining me. I'll answer that a long way around. You mentioned, "Underneath are the everlasting arms." That's Deuteronomy 33:27b (I had to look it up, but I knew it was the end of Deuteronomy). That was the mantra I said over and over again during Lucy Mac's birth! It came to me about halfway through first-stage labor and carried me through until she was born. Then two other passages sustained me while I adjusted to being a mom: one night when Lucy Mac was crying and I finally was so exhausted I cried too until she fell asleep in my arms and I was still crying, the passage came to me, "My grace is sufficient"; and then when I realized that parenting is a long-term adventure, I began to rely on the passage from James (1:5), "If any of you lacks wisdom, let her ask God, who gives to all generously....and it will be given her." So I'm used to passages of scripture swimming up from my unconscious to provide strength and comfort and hope.

Three years ago when I was waiting in the doctor's office before I knew for sure that the lump in my breast was malignant cancer (but I had a rather large suspicion), I found myself singing silently, "Have thine own way, Lord, have thine own way. Thou art the Potter, I am the clay. Mold me and make me after thy will while I am waiting, yielded and still." I think it was the last seven

---

[1] Nancy is Lucy's sister.

words that were the most poignant for me. Then as I was being wheeled down the hall the next day for surgery, I remembered Mama saying that she had felt very peaceful just before her surgery, as though God's presence was there with her. And almost immediately I found myself singing, "The lone wild bird in lofty flight is still with thee, nor leaves thy sight. And I am thine, I rest in thee. Great Spirit, come and rest in me." It was that sense of resting in God that was sustaining to me then. I even woke up in the recovery room singing that same hymn. The surgery was Thursday, and Saturday, the day I ended up going home, I woke up singing, "To God be the glory through Jesus the Son. I'll give God the glory, great things God has done. Praise the Lord, praise the Lord, let the earth hear your voice. Praise the Lord, praise the Lord, let all peoples rejoice. To God be the glory through Jesus the Son. I'll give God the glory, great things God has done." I know now that I changed the words all around to make them inclusive, but I didn't know it then. I was just singing a song of praise to God that swam up from my unconscious.

Now to this "adventure": there have been no similar scripture passages or hymns. The Friday after Gerry and I got the news about the cancer being in the bone, I went to Green Bough, a retreat center a couple of hours south of here. The woman who runs the center, Fay Key, did a little spiritual direction with me to the extent that I was unable to do much else than try to cope with the incredible pain. One passage she gave me was II Corinthians 4:7-18. A number of insights from that passage have continued to return to me helpfully. Let me copy the passage and underline the parts that were meaningful:

"But we have this treasure in clay jars, so that it may be made clear that <u>this extraordinary Power belongs to God and does not come from us</u>. <u>We are</u> afflicted in every way, but <u>not crushed</u>; perplexed, but <u>not driven to despair</u>; persecuted, but <u>not forsaken</u>; struck down, but <u>not destroyed</u>; always carrying in the body the death of Jesus, so that the life of Jesus may also be visible in our bodies. For while we live, we are always being given up to death for Jesus' sake, so that the life of Jesus may be made visible in our mortal flesh. So death is at work in us, but life in you.

"But just as we have the same spirit of faith that is in accordance with scripture--'I believed, and so I spoke'--we also believe, and so we speak, because we know that the one who raised the Lord Jesus will raise us also with Jesus, and will bring us with you into his presence. Yes, everything is for your sake, so that grace, as it extends to more and more people, may increase thanksgiving, to the glory of God.

"So we do not lose heart. Even though our outer nature is wasting away, our inner nature is being renewed day by day. For this slight momentary affliction is preparing us for an eternal weight of glory beyond all measure, because we look not at what can be seen but at what cannot be seen; for what can be seen is temporary, but what cannot be seen is eternal."

The main themes that come back to me are that the power that holds my life is God's, not mine; that by God's grace I have not felt crushed, driven to despair, forsaken, or destroyed (I've had people say to me, "Oh, you must be devastated." Well, no, I'm not --God's extraordinary grace!); that my hope is my experiences might enable grace to extend to more and more people, causing them to give thanks to God so that God is glorified; that my outer nature is wasting away, but again by God's grace I have at times (not so much recently) felt renewed day by day; and that in terms of eternity mine is a slight momentary affliction through which God's grace is preparing me for coming into God's eternal, loving presence. (I only pray that this affliction will also prepare Lucy Mac and Gerry for living more faithfully and trustingly with God.)

The other source of deep comfort and strength is the Teresa of Avila book you gave me. I have been trying to read a chapter a day, and each day I find myself in tears because she has named some experience for me or reminded me of a conviction I have been trying to live. For Teresa pain and suffering are not the enemy, as they seem to be in so much popular and even theological thinking today. For Teresa pain and suffering can be means to a deeper experience of God's love; they enable us to participate in the suffering of Christ. I have also found that my pain is a reminder of my solidarity with so many in the world who suffer, ache, and weep, as well as solidarity with the world itself that is groaning in travail; and then my pain moves me to pray, lifting us all up to God and reminding God of the promised shalom.

I suppose if there is a single prayer that returns repeatedly to my lips it is, "I surrender to your love, O God," or, "I entrust myself (body and soul) to you, O God." Today I also found myself praying that I will only to will God's will. It is this sense of surrender, renunciation, relinquishment that is my constant companion -- as well as an unshakable sense of God's overwhelming love.

In the last few days I have imaged myself as a piece of coral, part of a vast coral reef, and God is the ocean that is our life, our sustenance, our source of all that we need. Or I've imaged myself in an anteroom to God's throne room and I wait, longingly, to be admitted to God's presence; every now and then the door to the throne room opens, a hand reaches out, and God draws me into the rich, palpable darkness, holding me close in the divine bosom. An image from earlier in this adventure that continues to come back to me is that I am in God's womb, where all that I need is supplied through the umbilical cord, where the darkness is warm and life-giving, and where I am surrounded by love.

No mantras, no hymns -- but themes, images, words of a sister saint, and prayers, oh, so many prayers.

You wrote: "I don't know whether any of this makes sense." I would say the same to you; except I think enough of it does make sense, and I thank you for the opportunity to ponder and reflect and write. I'm trying to keep a journal every day or two, but it's also helpful to gather the themes and images together. I love you very much. Thanks for staying in touch.

The doctor today said that the hormone therapy isn't working and we'll start chemotherapy on Monday! I've shed lots of tears over that -- but, once more, I entrust myself to God's love!

Love,
Lucy

Letter #3

Dearest, dearest friends and family:

I cannot begin to thank you all for your cards, calls, and prayers. You have been angels--messengers from God, reminders of divine care and attentiveness. Thank you more than you can ever know. It's way past time for an update on my health, but in fact I've been in limbo for about two months. For those of you who don't know the progression of my therapy, I'll briefly recap. I tried two hormone therapies during the summer, neither of which worked. The doctor then shifted me to a chemotherapy called Taxol. After three rounds the doctor determined the Taxol wasn't working either and switched me to a different chemotherapy, Navelbine, which I was supposed to take every week. Soon after I started taking the Navelbine, I had a second occurrence of a bout with nausea, vomiting and diarrhea. Then in the last few weeks I've had to skip every other treatment of the chemotherapy due to a low white blood count, and then in addition I've had a third and fourth attack of the nausea, vomiting, and diarrhea. The doctor is miffed, doesn't think it's related to the chemotherapy, but has no idea what's causing the bouts. Meanwhile I'm losing weight and finding myself very weak from not eating nutritious food for days at a time. I've basically told the doctor I need a break from the chemotherapy to recover some energy and maybe a bit of "quality of life."

Now here's the latest news. With the support of my family, but not my doctor (he'll cooperate but he says he's not supportive), I'm planning to go to the Gerson Institute in Mexico, outside San Diego, for massive nutritional therapy. I'll leave Tuesday, Nov. 26, and return December 16. It's a three-week regimen, and my sister, Peggy, will accompany me. We've talked to a number of folks who have tried this kind of nutritional therapy and one man who

112

just returned from the Gerson Institute, and they all say they'd do it again.

We're not expecting a miracle cure, although we'd accept one with deep gratitude if such is God's will. I'm really looking for a boost to my immune system and a return to a more normal level of energy and strength. I'm not unwilling to resume chemotherapy once I return. At the present we're trying to discern God's will in the midst of low grade pain, almost constant weakness, and profound uncertainty--except this visit to the Gerson Institute has fallen into place so smoothly I can only call it providential.

Your prayers are a source of comfort and strength. Please, continue to hold us up.

Much love,
Lucy

Dear friends and family,

It is <u>way</u> past time for an update. Again let me begin with a heartfelt thank you for your prayers, cards, calls, gifts, visits, meals, and all the many ways you've supported and encouraged my family and me. You have truly incarnated Paul's words to believers, "Bear one another's burdens and so fulfill the law of Christ." I am especially grateful for your prayers. As I have said many times, when I get discouraged, I find that I can relax into your thoughts and prayers and feel them (you) holding me close to God's heart.

There is evidence that the tumors continue to grow -- X-rays that show slightly increased deterioration of the bones in my upper left leg, recent numbness in the lower right half of my chin. The doctor is sure that these symptoms are not immediately life-threatening, and I have opted for the time being not to undergo radiation to try and shrink the tumors. Radiation can have a whole range of debilitating and/or unpleasant side effects.

I am not following the strict Gerson regimen I learned in Mexico because I could not eat enough calories to maintain my weight at a livable level. I have, however, continued to eat organic foods. I remain on a low sodium, low fat, restricted sugar diet -- vegetarian except for fresh white-fish filet, two to four times a week.

This semester I have, by the grace of God, been able to teach two sections of the introductory preaching and worship course. I have twelve students in each section. Teaching has been a joy for me. And most of the time I am able to reserve enough energy for my family. Only on a few evenings have I been too exhausted to read to Lucy Mac before bedtime, hear her prayers, and sing the current going-to-bed songs. She continues to be a typical seven year-old, concerned about her Mommy and aware of the peculiarities associated with my being sick, but not, I keep praying, depressed, angry, or scarred by my illness. Gerry, from my point of view, continues to be a gift from God for whom I am daily thankful.

Some wonderful news is that my book is out: *Sharing the Word: Preaching in the Roundtable Church*, published by Westminster/John Knox Press. I am proud of it. They did a particularly nice job of the cover.

As I learn to live not day to day but hour by hour with the particular ups and downs of pain and weariness, I am growing more aware of and grateful for such affirmations as "I believe in God....I believe in Jesus Christ....I believe in the Holy Spirit, the holy catholic church, the communion of saints, the forgiveness of sins, the resurrection of the body, and the life everlasting." Each affirmation points to a reality or network of realities that more and more deeply grounds my faith. God is becoming in the past few months the One I know in the Jesus of Scripture, whose love and life have been poured into my heart through the Holy Spirit. I have my whole life long believed in the sovereign transcendence of God. Now I am experiencing the deep immanence of God within me, the incarnation in me of God's life so that in terms of that life it is no longer I who live but Christ within me. Especially I am aware that this life within me that arises as the gift of the Holy Spirit is everlasting life and cannot be snuffed out. This life draws me deep into God's love and into the bonds that constitute our life together as the community of believers. To die is gain--to be fully alive in God's unfathomably loving presence. But I believe I am not right now being called to die but to live this earthly life as abundantly as I am able -- loving those I have been given to love, teaching and learning from co-learners in the classroom, and glorifying God, sometimes with my doing but more often with my being.

Love,

Lucy

Chapter 4

Lucy's Last Five Days, reported by Marilyn Washburn

On Saturday morning (July 12, 1997) Lucy greeted me with the announcement that she was ready to die. I asked her what was left for her to do and she said, "Nothing. Nothing." A few seconds later she said, "I have to tell Chuck I can't teach this Fall." I asked if she wanted to call him or ask him to come over, and she said, "I can't; I'll only cry." Later, she asked me to talk to him. Chuck came to see her. He told me that he told her he loved her, and he brought her a copy of his book. They sat in silence for a long time and then he prayed with her before he left. She told me that he had come, that they had shared silence and prayer, and that it was a good visit.

We sat in silence for a few minutes, Lucy grasping my hand and struggling to breathe, me kneeling beside her bed. She asked me, "What will happen? What will it be like to die?" I told her that I thought she would get more and more sleepy. She said, "I'm not afraid." I asked her whom she wanted to be with her when she died, other than Gerry and Lucy Mac. She said, "Dean and Louie," trying not to cry, so I prompted her and said, "And your family?" She nodded and said, "I think that's why this family reunion is so important to me."[1] After a few minutes, she asked me to read to her the last chapter of the Mrs. Pollifax book, a mystery novel. The tone of our visit lightened and after we finished the book, she said she would like to sleep.

On Sunday morning, Lucy had some fever, and she became

---

[1] The Rose family has a reunion every summer and had planned to have it in Decatur the following week-end.

116

much more weak and short of breath. Throughout the afternoon, in her "dreaming," she talked of being "in the heart of Jesus." By late afternoon Gerry sensed that Lucy might not be able to continue through the week, and made the decision to call the family. During the evening she rallied a little and Gerry told her that her parents were on the way. She talked of them and said, "I'm so glad. I'm so glad." Gerry told Lucy Mac that we thought Lucy would only live a few days....she shouted, "A few days?!" Lucy called Jana to say, "Goodbye." Gerry and Jana discussed the funeral sermon. Lucy wrote letters to Dean and Louie. She struggled for a long time to compose a letter to the students at the Seminary, "I want to bless them, somehow," but she could not find the words.

Most of the night Lucy rambled incoherently, mixing instructions about where things should be put away, bits of conversation with friends, fragments of Scripture and prayers.

<u>Monday morning</u> I was at work at Emory Family & Preventive Medical Center. In the early afternoon, Lucy's parents arrived. Chuck came with Rebecca Parker, Don Fierbach, Dana Campbell and Jim Hudnut-Buemler -- to celebrate the Lord's Supper.

Peggy, Lucy's sister, arrived and she and Lucy spent some time together. Not long afterwards, Lucy began her rambling speech again, and then lapsed into a coma, no longer responsive to our attempts to talk to her or gently rouse her. Catherine Gonzalez came by to visit. We put the earphones of the tape recorder beside her ear and played tapes her family and friends had made of the Psalms.

In the early evening the Community of Hospitality came to pray and sing. I sat with Lucy Mac on Gerry's bed. At times I thought she was trying to sing too, moving her mouth in rhythm with the words. After they each said goodbye to her, they lingered a few minutes on the front porch.

In the late evening, Lucy awakened with enough strength to talk with us again, and take some sorbets.

<u>Tuesday about 4:00 a.m.</u> Ann Connor awakened Peggy

and me saying that Lucy had said that she thought she only had two hours to live. She asked that her parents be called. When they arrived, Mrs. Rose asked if she would like to be sung to, and her parents sang a medley of childhood songs. Dr. Rose suggested that they sing hymns through the alphabet (as they used to do when traveling as a family), which they did. At one point Lucy said, "When I get to that beautiful shore, I'm going to drink and drink and drink." (She was thirsty much of the time and we had continually to give her water.) Later she said, "I've heard that you see people when you die and I want to see Teresa of Avila." Others in the room added names of family members, and Peggy said, "And Jesus." "No," Lucy responded, "You don't get to see him until the second day." As the time neared the end of two hours and it became clear that Lucy was not going to die immediately, she apologized for getting everyone up and said it was a "bum steer."

Tuesday p.m. Tammy, from Hospice, came and gave Lucy a bath. She was gentle and attentive and the bath was stimulating and energizing for Lucy. Catherine and Jeanne stopped by briefly but Lucy was too fatigued to visit long. She was alert most of the afternoon and asked me to read Jesus' farewell discourse from John's Gospel to her.

In the early evening the nurse, Kim, came by. She did some therapeutic touching to ease Lucy's pain, and told her she thought she could die if she could only relax enough to sleep. Later, in the kitchen, Kim told us the same thing and asked if anyone had given Lucy permission to die.

Lucy called each of us in to speak to her individually. She told me she was going to try to sleep and was not sure she would wake up, and wanted to thank me for being her friend. Gerry wanted to be sure she had heard the inscription Chuck had written to her in his book which read, "For Lucy, a disciple of Jesus and a saint of the Church. Thank you for being my friend and colleague. Chuck." When he read it to her, Lucy shook her head and said, "I wasn't that nice to him." The Community again came

118

to sing and pray. Lucy was awake and alert, joined them from time to time and made requests for songs. After they left, Lucy and I talked briefly about how to help her relax. I promised to give her the medication she needed to be comfortable. For the first part of the night, I held her hand, and tried to comfort her when her "dreaming" seemed to be keeping her awake. B came in to spell me about 11:30.

Wednesday 2:45 a.m. Lucy said in a clear voice, "Praise be to God, praise be to God; Glory be to God, glory be to God." B and I changed places. After a few minutes Lucy asked, "Is God in control?" I began an answer, "Yes, yes, God is in control," when she interrupted me saying deliberately and between gasps for air, "The theodicy debate is only an attempt to protect God. God does not need our protection. We must continue to live in the paradox." I realized that the question was a rhetorical one, that the litany of praise was probably how Lucy began her classes, and that she was once again teaching. For the next four hours, as her energy and gasping permitted, she talked about preaching. She outlined Fred Craddock's categories. She tried to give me some examples of how she incorporated stories from movies into sermons, but abandoned the attempt when I confessed I had not seen the movies. She told me to preach about prayer. She said she had never preached about grief, and that I must give that subject some thought and attention. She said, "I would appreciate your insights about preaching." I declined, explaining that I have no insights and that I was very intimidated by the invitation to discuss preaching with her. She pressed me, saying again she wanted my insights.

So I explained to her that whenever I am in the pulpit, I realize I *really* believe what I say I believe about God Almighty meeting people through the words I speak. I told her that what I do as a physician is only to postpone death, that what I do as a preacher is *really* about saving lives and that it is so awesome a calling that I am deeply and profoundly fearful. Throughout this very confessional moment, she gripped my hand and nodded her encouragement to finish what I was saying. When I was through, I asked her if she had any suggestions for someone like me. She answered, "That's a very good question," and she encouraged me to find people to support me "in dealing with the texts and the issues." She told me that when she preached regularly she always tried to be a part of such a group, and how one such group had helped her "develop (her) speaking voice." Just before 7:00 a.m., when she had been breathing quietly and staring ahead for several minutes, I said, "Lucy, I have the feeling you have just given me your Fall course in homiletics." She smiled and said, "I think maybe so." She lapsed again into the vivid dreaming and rambling talking, during which I could understand only a few short phrases or single words.

Next morning, Murphy came by and sat with us for a few minutes. Lucy asked about Murphy's daughter, Hannah.

(I went home for a few hours.) Chuck called me in mid-afternoon, saying Lucy's breathing had changed.

By the time I arrived, the "old" breathing pattern had returned, and again, we took turns waiting with her. About 6:00 p.m., I noticed she was cold and clammy and that her pulse was very high. I asked Dakin to confirm my suspicion that Lucy was in shock, and once again we called family and friends to say we thought Lucy would live only a few more hours.

Friends came and sat together on the front porch. We asked them to sing so they could be heard down the hall and we opened the door so Lucy could hear them. She asked Ann to read the liturgical reading for the day, and joined her with the doxological response "Glory be to the Father...." Then, again, she lapsed into the dreaming and wandering speech. About 10:00 p.m. she said, "I do so want to die, but my body and God are not together." (After this I was gone for two hours).

About 3:00 a.m. Thursday morning, Lucy sent Ann to get me. She had told me several times before that she did not want to assign Ann the role of health professional at her death, that she was asking me to do that so Ann could be free to be her friend. When

120

we returned to her room, she tried to explain to Ann, calling me the "lead carpenter." Shortly after we had settled down again, she tried to sing the phrase "When we meet on that beautiful shore...." but could not breathe to finish and said to me, "How about a song?" Ann began singing a song from the Psalms about God's presence with us and the chorus, "Be not afraid, for I am with you always. Come follow me and I will give you rest." Lucy relaxed a little and after a few verses nodded to us that we could stop.

Several times during the night, she called my name, stroked my cheek and ran her fingers through my hair. It was tender, comforting, very maternal, as if she were trying to comfort *me* in *my* pain. About 5:30 a.m., she again roused momentarily from her dreaming and said very deliberately, "The important thing to me is that our God is so magnificent....came to walk among us....knows the depths of our suffering....and loves us and loves us and loves us...." About 5:40 a.m., she became very agitated, pulled the oxygen tube from her nose, groped for my hand and face. I realized she could no longer breathe at all. Ann awakened Gerry while I told her it would be a few more minutes. When Gerry held her, she relaxed and began breathing shallowly and peacefully. He told her he loved her, awakened Lucy Mac who came in and kissed her and told Lucy she loved her. Ann and I gathered Dean and Louie, B, Nancy and Peggy, and called Dakin. Gerry rocked Lucy Mac in his lap, holding Lucy in his other arm. Lucy's breathing slowed, and stopped at 6:02 a.m. The group stood by her bed and sang the Doxology.

Appendix

Item 1

Biographical Sketch of Lucy Atkinson Rose

Lucy Atkinson Rose was born in Bristol, Virginia, February 15, 1947, the daughter of Rev. & Mrs. Ben Lacy Rose. She had two sisters older and one brother younger than she. Another brother was born when Lucy was five years old, but he lived only three weeks. She attended public schools in Bristol, Virginia, Wilmington, North Carolina and Richmond, Virginia, and graduated *cum laude* from Agnes Scott College in Decatur, Georgia, in 1968. Receiving a Master of Arts in Teaching (MAT) degree from Emory University in Atlanta in 1969, she taught English in Atlanta's Grady and Douglass high schools and coached basketball from 1969-71.

After a brief period of study at Cambridge University in England, she returned to the United States and attended Union Theological Seminary in Richmond, Virginia. During the summer of 1972, she was summer assistant to the minister of Bethesda Presbyterian Church, Aberdeen, North Carolina. She also served as Intern Student-in-Ministry in First Presbyterian Church, Rocky Mount, North Carolina, from 1973-74.

When she graduated from Union Theological Seminary in Virginia in 1975 with a Doctor of Ministry (D.Min.) degree, she was awarded a fellowship for further graduate work, which she delayed using until 1977. She was ordained a minister of the Word and Sacrament by Fayetteville Presbytery of the Presbyterian Church U.S. on February 16, 1975 and was installed on that same date as associate pastor of First Presbyterian Church, Sanford, North Carolina. She served there until 1977 when she resigned in order to use the fellowship from UTS to do graduate study in the field of homiletics at Duke University. While studying in the Duke Divinity School, she served as Stated Supply of the Summerville Presbyterian Church, Lillington, North Carolina.

After receiving a Master of Theology (Th.M.) degree from Duke Divinity School in 1978, she accepted a call to the John Calvin Presbyterian Church in Salisbury, North Carolina. She was installed as pastor of the John Calvin Church where she served for five years.

In 1983 she was invited to become assistant professor of Homiletics and Worship in Columbia Theological Seminary in Decatur, Georgia, and began teaching there in September. On July 27, 1985 she married Fitzgerald (Gerry) M. Cook in the Clifton Presbyterian Church in Decatur, and on May 28, 1989, a daughter, Lucy McIlwaine Cook, was born to them.

Lucy enjoyed puzzles and there were very few that she could not solve. She found special delight in difficult jig-saw puzzles She also found great pleasure in making things with her hands, such as small paper boxes and three-dimensional Christmas cards. She was an excellent seamstress and often made clothes for herself and her daughter.

Lucy loved languages. Hebrew and Greek, which were required subjects at the seminary where she studied, fascinated her, and when she went to Palestine and Egypt in 1983, she learned the basics of Arabic script.

Lucy enjoyed preaching and preached regularly in churches in the Atlanta area. She was a popular speaker and worship leader at summer conferences and retreats.

Lucy knew by heart many of the hymns of the church and many passages of Scripture. When she was a child, her parents offered their children five cents for each verse of a hymn or of Scripture they would learn. Lucy's journal reveals that the memory of these songs and verses rose to sustain her in her times of need.

Lucy was member of two families, one into which she was born and one which she and Gerry formed. In both families she was loved *by* and returned love *to* each member, but at times Lucy

123

was not a saint as that word is popularly understood today. She was a human being who had her faults. When she was out-of-sorts or when things did not go as she thought they should, Lucy could be very impatient and even short with those she loved. What was exemplary about her was her abiding faith in God's sovereign love and goodness.

Soon after she began teaching at Columbia Seminary, Lucy joined the national Academy of Homiletics, and she served as its president in 1994-95. While continuing to teach, she earned the Ph.D. degree at Emory University in Atlanta. The degree was awarded on May 8, 1995. Her doctoral work in Theology and Literature, performed under the supervision of Dr. Fred B. Craddock, resulted in her thesis being published by Westminster/ John Knox Press under the title of *Sharing The Word: Preaching in the Roundtable Church.* She was co-editor with Dr. Jana L. Childers of three other books, *The Abingdon Women's Preaching Annual, Series 1, Year A; The Abingdon Women's Preaching Annual, Series 1, Year B* and *The Abingdon Women's Preaching Annual, Series 1, Year C,* published by Abingdon Press.

On April 3, 1996, Lucy was installed as tenured associate professor of Preaching and Worship at Columbia Theological Seminary.

Although Lucy served as a theological seminary professor for fourteen years, she never lost her love for the parish. In her professional resume she wrote: "For as long as I can remember, I have been committed to the work of the local church. After my graduation from college, I taught high school English in two Atlanta public schools and was active in Central Presbyterian Church, Atlanta. While in Seminary and on the Richmond campus, I continued active membership in my home church, teaching a youth Sunday School class. My initial introduction to the ministry came in the summer of 1972 when I served as assistant to the minister in the Bethesda Presbyterian Church in Aberdeen, North Carolina. From October, 1972, until December, 1973, I served as student interim in First Presbyterian Church of Rocky Mount,

North Carolina. I was ordained to the gospel ministry to serve as associate pastor in the First Presbyterian Church of Sanford, North Carolina. In that capacity I had across-the-board responsibilities in leadership, in worship and visitation, and particular responsibilities in youth work and Christian Education. After a year of study at Duke Divinity School, I went to Salisbury, North Carolina, where I served as pastor of the John Calvin Presbyterian Church. In June 1983 I joined the faculty of Columbia Theological Seminary as assistant professor of worship and preaching. In many ways I see my work here at the seminary as a continuation of my commitment to the local church."

In June 1993, when doctors determine that a lump in her breast was malignant, she had a mastectomy. Several weeks of chemotherapy followed. When classes began in September, her hair had fallen out as a result of the chemotherapy, so she wore a hat to class. As a gesture of support, the students declared "Hat Day" in her honor and on that day every person at the seminary wore a hat.

At the end of the chemotherapy both she and her doctor believed that she was free of cancer. Unfortunately, in June 1996, she found that the cancer had returned and was quite wide-spread. It had spread into the bones of her legs, arms, back and face. Under doctor's care, she tried several treatments, but none seemed to help, the cancer continued to spread and her pain increased. In Fall 1996, she spent three weeks at the Gerson Therapy Center in Baja California, Mexico, which advocates diet therapy for cancer, but that experiment neither stopped the spread of the cancer nor ended her pain.

In her journal Lucy is not ashamed to confess that, during her bout with cancer, she cried often. One is reminded of Viktor Frankl's words about the victims of Auschwitz, "There was no need to be ashamed of tears, for tears bore witness that one had the greatest of courage, the courage to suffer."

During the academic year 1996-97, Lucy taught at Columbia Seminary, even though she was in almost constant pain. Chuck

Campbell, her colleague in the homiletics department, said at her funeral, "Last Spring Lucy taught every class except the very last one. And she was something to watch. She would shuffle into the classroom with the help of Gerry or her brother -- pale, thin, frail and probably in more pain than any of us can imagine. She would sit down, hunched over in the special chair she had. And when I knelt beside her to check about the class, she would whisper, 'If I can't get through it, can you take it?' 'Sure,' I replied. But I soon learned that I would never be called on. As soon as the class began, Lucy would move to the front of the room. And before I knew it, the color had come back to her face and she would be writing on the board, waving her arms, telling jokes, even sitting up on the table. It was an amazing transformation."

After the close of the seminary's academic year in May, Lucy spent most of her time at home under the care of her dear friend, Marilyn Washburn, who is a practicing physician (as well as an ordained minister). Marilyn spent many hours with Lucy and administered the medicines she needed.

Lucy died at her home at 185 Mead Road in Decatur, at 6:02 a.m on July 17, 1997, surrounded by family and friends. She was lucid up to an hour or less before her death. Her funeral was conducted in the Decatur Presbyterian Church on July 19, 1997 with interment following in the Decatur Cemetery. Columbia Theological Seminary conducted a memorial service on September 12, 1997. Her obituary read as follows:

"Rev. Dr. Lucy A. Rose, age 50, of Decatur died July 17, 1997. She is survived by her husband, Mr. Gerry Cook; daughter, Miss Lucy McIlwaine Cook, Decatur; parents, Dr. & Mrs. Ben L. (Anne) Rose, Richmond, VA; sisters, Mrs. Nancy Rose Vosler, St. Louis, MO & Mrs. Peggy Rose Day, Mystic, CT; brother, Mr. Ben L. Rose Jr., Richmond, VA.; also Louie Dowis and Dean Shirley, both of Decatur. A memorial service will be held Saturday afternoon at 2:00 at Decatur Presbyterian Church. Rev. Currie Burris will officiate."

Appendix

Item 2

Identification of Persons Mentioned in This Book

AB. Short -- co-founder of Community of Hospitality; husband of Ann Connor.

Allison Mawle -- mother of Lucy Mac's friend, Jonathan.

Anne Stevens -- pastor, attorney and former student of Lucy.

Ann Connor -- close friend of Lucy; co-founder of Community of Hospitality; mother of Egan.

Aunt Alice -- beloved aunt of Lucy, Mrs. W. M. Thompson.

B -- Ben Rose Jr., Lucy's brother.

Ben L. Rose -- Lucy's father.

Ben C. Johnson -- colleague of Lucy on the faculty of Columbia Seminary.

Becca Vines -- Gerry's sister.

Becky Hanks -- friend of Lucy.

Berta Story -- friend of Lucy.

Beth Thompson -- friend of Lucy in Clifton Presbyterian Church.

Bobby Vines -- Gerry's brother-in-law.

Catherine Gonzalez -- colleague of Lucy on the faculty of Columbia Seminary.

Chuck Campbell -- Charles. L. Campbell, colleague of Lucy on the faculty of Columbia Seminary.

Cousin Claiborne Jones -- first cousin of Lucy.

127

Currie Burris -- pastor of Clifton Presbyterian Church, Decatur.

Dakin Cook -- Gerry's brother.

Dana Campbell -- wife of Chuck Campbell.

Dean Shirley -- friend with whom Lucy and Gerry shared their home.

Debbi Neuroth -- Gerry's sister.

Don Fierbach -- student of Lucy at Columbia Seminary.

Doris Chandler -- former student of Lucy.

Egan Short -- Lucy Mac's friend; dau. of Ann Connor & AB.

Elaine Rhodes -- classmate of Lucy at Union Seminary.

Erskine Clarke -- colleague of Lucy on the faculty of Columbia Seminary.

Fay Key -- dear friend of Lucy; co-director of Green Bough Retreat Center.

Fred B. Craddock -- professor at Emory University under whom Lucy performed her Ph.D. work.

Garcia, Dr. -- doctor at the Gerson Institute.

Gerry Cook -- Lucy's husband.

Isabel -- Lucy Mac's dog.

Jana Childers -- colleague of Lucy in the Academy of Homiletics.

Jeanne S. Moessner -- colleague of Lucy at Columbia Seminary.

Jim Hudnut-Beumler -- colleague of Lucy at Columbia Seminary.

Jim Watkins -- friend of Lucy in Community of Hospitality.

Joan Delaplane -- colleague of Lucy in the Academy of Homiletics.

Jonathan Lowe -- Lucy Mac's best friend at school.

Joy Pruett -- former student of Lucy.

Justo Gonzalez -- husband of Catherine Gonzalez.

Kathleen Murdock -- friend of Lucy.

Kathleen O'Connor -- colleague of Lucy on the faculty of
Columbia Seminary.

Lauren Moore -- former student of Lucy.

Lisa Ryan -- friend of Lucy in Clifton Presbyterian Church.

Louie Dowis -- friend with whom Lucy and Gerry shared their
home.

Lucy Atkinson McIlwaine -- Lucy's great aunt for whom she &
Lucy Mac were named.

Lucy Mac -- Lucy McIlwaine Cook, daughter of Lucy and
Gerry.

Lynnsay Buehler -- friend of Lucy at Green Bough; wife of Rob
Townes.

Marilyn Washburn -- physician friend of Lucy who attended her
faithfully during her last days.

Mary Bailey Davis -- friend of Lucy and mother of Murphy.

Mike Vosler -- husband of Lucy's sister, Nancy.

Murphy Davis -- long-time friend of Lucy from summers in
Montreat, North Carolina..

Nancy Vosler -- Lucy's sister.

Oo (Elise Slay) Finkner -- long-time friend of Lucy from days
together in Richmond VA.

Paul Franklyn -- friend of Lucy.

Peggy Day -- Lucy's sister.

Pete Caruthers -- former colleague of Lucy at Columbia Seminary.

Peteet, Dr. David -- of Meridian Medical Group; Lucy's doctor.

Rebecca Parker -- colleague of Lucy at Columbia Seminary.

Rebekah Stone -- friend of Lucy in Community of Hospitality.

Rob Townes -- friend of Lucy at Green Bough; husband of Lynnsay Buehler.

Ruth Anne Foote -- friend of Lucy in Clifton Presbyterian Church.

Sally Brown & Peter -- Lucy's assistant for CTS classes in the Spring of 1997; Peter is Sally's husband.

Steve Bullinger -- co-director of Green Bough Retreat Center.

Swami -- friend of Lucy in Community of Hospitality.

Tolly -- younger brother of Lucy who lived only three weeks.

Tom Long -- former professor of homiletics at Columbia Seminary; friend of Lucy.

Twins -- younger siblings of Lucy who died at birth.

Wade P. Huie Jr. -- colleague of Lucy on the faculty of Columbia Seminary.

Walter Brueggemann -- colleague of Lucy on the faculty of Columbia Seminary.

Whitney Bryant -- friend of Lucy in Community of Hospitality.